What the experts about *Making Se Leasehold Property*

'This book provides excellent advice for the growing number of people buying flats. It gives a compelling account of the leasehold system, with its curiously British characteristics that date back to the Norman Conquest.'

Henry Tricks, former residential property editor,
Financial Times

'*Making Sense of Leasehold Property* is an invaluable source of practical help and advice for the millions of owners of leasehold properties, many of whom can benefit from an extension of their lease, purchase of the freehold, or the new right to manage legislation. Written in plain English, leasehold expert Kat Callo sets out a step-by-step guide for anyone wanting to pursue their rights as a leaseholder and enhance the value of their property. The author has practical experience of dealing with leasehold problems and highlights how to avoid the pitfalls and increase the chances of success. This book is a must for all owners of leasehold property.'

Lorna Bourke, former personal finance editor,
the *Daily Telegraph*, *The Times* and *The Independent*

What the experts say about
Making Sense of Leasehold Property

'Leasehold property used to be complex and obscure, but recent reforms have transformed it into a nightmare. Should you enfranchise, fight for the right to manage, or go for an extension? All leaseholders will be faced with these decisions sooner or later, and Kat Callo's book is a valuable guide through the minefield.'

Chris Partridge, freelance residential property journalist

'It is really useful to have such an interesting and well-researched book on the leasehold system written by such a dedicated and well-informed professional such as Kat Callo. The Federation of Private Residents' Associations supports Kat, in that she understands and promotes leaseholders working together to achieve common benefit for all. This book will certainly increase the knowledge base in an important way amongst the leaseholders, residents' associations and resident management companies that we represent and amongst other stakeholders in the area of leaseholder rights.'

Robert Levene, Chief Executive,
Federation of Private Residents' Associations

'This book is not only a useful and practical guide for leaseholders, but also contains fascinating insight from Kat Callo into understanding the leasehold system in an easily-accessible format.'

Nicolas Shulman, Founder, *News On The Block* magazine

Making Sense of Leasehold Property

Kat Callo

Making Sense of Leasehold Property
by Kat Callo

© 2005 Kat Callo
Reprinted 2006

Lawpack Publishing Limited
76–89 Alscot Road
London SE1 3AW

www.lawpack.co.uk

ISBN: 1-904053-12-2
ISBN: 978-1-904053-12-5

Exclusion of Liability and Disclaimer

Contents

About the author

Kat Callo is an international strategy consultant, writer and leading advocate of leaseholder rights in England and Wales. She is founding director of Rosetta Consulting Ltd, a strategy consultancy that advises leaseholders, solicitors, surveyors, government bodies and other clients on collective enfranchisement, lease extensions, right to manage and related leasehold subjects. Before incorporating Rosetta, Kat worked for 17 years at Reuters, initially as a foreign correspondent and later as a media executive at the global headquarters in London. An Anglo-American born in New York, her journalistic postings with Reuters took her to Belgium, the Philippines, Hong Kong and Vietnam, where she set up Reuters' first Hanoi news bureau in 1990. Kat also did reporting for Reuters from Afghanistan, Cambodia, Guam, New Caledonia and other locations in the Asia-Pacific region. She later set up a number of new information and news products and services while working on the commercial side of Reuters back in London, and served as senior vice president in charge of a global media business. Kat is a graduate of Columbia University School of Journalism and London Business School. She and her husband, Peter Wilson-Smith, and their boys, Henry and Benedict, divide their time between London and Suffolk.

Acknowledgements

This book would not have been possible without assistance from many people. I am grateful for all the help extended to me by many experts in the area of leasehold property, including skilled professional advisors and the many consumers who have had to struggle with the outdated aspects of the system. Any mistakes in this book are my own responsibility.

Charlotte Sewell, Jackie Jowett, Renu Basra and their team at the Office of the Deputy Prime Minister provided valuable help during my research. I am deeply grateful to Siobhan McGrath and her colleagues at the Residential Property Tribunal Service. Jerry Sharma, Michael Ross, Aileen Hamilton-Farey, Sheila Partridge and Yoro Edmond provided crucial assistance in understanding the workings of Leasehold Valuation Tribunals and Rent Assessment Panels.

Peter Haler has provided generous assistance and important inspiration at the Leasehold Advisory Service. His team of experts, Anthony Essien, Nicholas Kissen and other advisors there offered limitless patience and helpfulness when I contacted them with questions about leaseholder rights. My thanks also go to Chris Humphreys, who helped me during his secondment to the Office of the Deputy Prime Minister.

I am grateful to Yvonne Taylor and her colleagues at Companies House for helping me with research on resident management and right to manage companies.

I gathered crucial information for this book from solicitors and barristers that specialise in leasehold reform, including Alan Edwards and Swita Chandarana at Alan Edwards & Co., John Spencer-Silver at Rooks Rider, Willem Baars and Rupert Rokeby-Johnson at Rokeby Johnson Baars, Damien Greenish at Pemberton Greenish, Jennifer Israel at Jennifer Israel

& Co. and Jonathan Small at Falcon Chambers. I am grateful for the opportunity to have learned from their valuable knowledge and expertise. Several surveyors who are experts on collective enfranchisement helped and inspired me in preparing this guide, including Mark Wilson, Prosper Marr-Johnson, Tim Martin, Guy Hollamby, Michael Tims, Owen Grainger and Jonathan Harris. They also showed good humour each time I oversimplified the freehold valuation calculation with my own ten-word back-of-envelope formula.

An essential ingredient for this book was the many stories told to me by leaseholders across the country. They are too numerous to list here, but special thanks go to Karen Wolman, Heather Darnell, Tara Gay-Nealon, Reay Tannahill, Annabel Cary, Tony Hidden, Michael Fuke, Philippa Ingram, Roland Rench and Gloria Goldring. I am also grateful to friends and colleagues around the world who helped me compare England's leasehold system with apartment ownership in other countries. My deep gratitude goes to Marie-France Sevestre, Ivan Newman, Nancy Payne, Leslie Adler, Antonia Sharpe, Emma Robson, John Kohut, Markus Payer, Wendy Lubetkin, Gerry Obara, Heather Harper, Scott James and Lisa Sands. The leaseholders of Burnham Court, London W2 deserve special mention for inspiring me regarding the quest to gain control of one's destiny by buying one's building freehold.

Justin Downes provided friendship and invaluable advice on new ways to solve problems created by the outdated aspects of the leasehold system. Martyn Reed helped me by bringing London Business School-style rigour to an analysis of changing consumer trends in this area of home ownership.

The Federation of Private Residents' Associations assisted me repeatedly with information and encouragement. For this I extend warm thanks to Muriel Guest Smith and to Robert Levine. My appreciation also goes to Philippa Turner and John Peartree. Special thanks are reserved for Lord Coleraine for describing to me the fascinating debates in the House of Lords during the passage of enfranchisement legislation following the election in 1992 of John Major. At Jordans Limited, Rachel Wheatley, Simon Groves, Joe Cressy and Nichola Webb were generous in their assistance and encouragement. Alex Greenslade, Anna Bailey, Andrew Lyndon-Skeggs and Bernie Wales helped me by sharing a common goal to serve leaseholders. Special thanks go to Neil Manning and Martin Bikhit.

I am grateful to the many people who helped me spread the word about leaseholder rights, including Anne Spackman, Catherine Riley and Susan Emmet at *The Times*, Henry Tricks and Alison Beard at the *Financial Times*, Janice Morley, Jane Barry and Mira Bar-Hillel at the *Evening Standard*, and Nic Shulman and Mark Ronan at *News On The Block*. Chris Partridge at *The Independent* deserves a special mention for applying an eagle eye to the book manuscript and sharing the anecdote that King Henry II granted land to a Suffolk tenant for performing a leap, whistle and fart at court each Christmas. Julie Purkiss at Cadogan Insurance Services and Lynn East were also instrumental in helping me to inform leaseholders on a national basis. Antonia Sharpe, Cathie Calvert and Roz Hanna gave me invaluable advice on how best to get the message across to leaseholders and other major stakeholders.

I am grateful for the support and dynamic feedback that was continually provided by Jamie Ross, my editor at Lawpack Publishing.

My mother, Sue Callo, was a huge help, especially when she repeatedly expressed amazement at outdated aspects of the leasehold system. My father, Joe Callo, and Sally provided continual encouragement in the writing of this book, by reminding me of the ability of the individual to change the system.

I could not have written this book without the love and support of my husband, Peter Wilson-Smith, and our boys, Henry and Benedict. They have shown great humour and understanding during the many moments when I appeared unwilling to talk about anything beyond enfranchisement and other leaseholder rights.

Foreword

If you own a flat in England or Wales, the chances are that it will be leasehold. Despite this fact, the leasehold system remains a complete mystery to the vast majority of flat owners. Very few homeowners read their lease or even keep a copy, and there is little appreciation of the relative burdens and obligations of the leasehold system. To the average owner of a flat, the leasehold system remains something distant and impenetrable, akin to income tax assessment or the mysteries of VAT.

Making Sense of Leasehold Property has been a long time coming. This book provides a unique and valuable guide through the thickets of leasehold law, written in simple and practical terms by a flat owner for flat owners. This essential handbook works from the simple question, 'What does a leaseholder need to know?' As a flat owner, you may not want to be a leaseholder, but in England and Wales it is essentially the only game in town and you need to know the rules.

Peter Haler, Chief Executive, Leasehold Advisory Service

INTRODUCTION

Why England is different from everywhere else

A puzzling property system

A newcomer arriving in the United Kingdom is often baffled when buying a flat. Faced with the prospect of paying a large amount of money for an apartment in central London, the buyer is puzzled to see in the sales documentation that the flat has a specific number of years left on the lease, say, 60. It comes as a further shock to learn that the purchaser does not actually own the property, but rather has simply bought a lease that provides permission to use it for a time. More worrying still is the realisation that this property is a diminishing asset, the net market value of which decreases as the term of the lease expires.

All of this flies in the face of widely-held consumer perceptions in other industrialised nations: that buying a property equals ownership and that one should expect the net market value of a well-maintained home to appreciate, not depreciate, over time.

Welcome to the bewildering world of leasehold and freehold, a property system virtually unique to England and Wales, with origins dating back 1,000 years. This book presents a guide to the leasehold and freehold system, with all its peculiarities, and provides the consumer with tips on how to make the best of an imperfect legislative environment that continues, despite reforms, to borrow heavily from the feudal age.

The leasehold system represents an awkward halfway house between owning and renting. It bears little resemblance to the residential property system existing in most other industrialised countries. If you live in an apartment building in New York, you are likely either to rent your apartment from its owner or else to own the unit yourself. If your apartment is a so-called 'co-op' or 'condo', then not only do you own your unit in perpetuity, but also you are a joint owner of the building along with fellow residents.

Move across the Atlantic and one finds a similar system through much of Western Europe. If you occupy a flat in Rome, you will be a renter or else you will own the unit according to a similar condominium system as that which exists in the United States. This makes you and other residents collectively responsible for the upkeep of your building and the grounds. In France, this type of apartment ownership is called 'co-propriété', or co-ownership, which means that you own your unit as part of the collective group of residents. Your ownership of the apartment is total and forever, so you can pass on the property, if you wish, to your heirs.

It is surprising to international observers that flats in central London often cost more than equivalent units in major cities in other countries, and yet purchase does not result in full ownership. Indeed, the term 'flat owner' in England is usually a misnomer, since a person buying a leasehold flat is only buying a so-called interest in the unit and is not by any means the complete owner. Despite the fact that 'flat owner' is technically a misleading term, this book will use it for the sake of simplicity.

In England and Wales, if one owns a house or a flat, it is not possible – technically speaking – ever to be the full owner of the land itself. This is because, dating back to the Norman Conquest in 1066, only the Crown can actually own land. All other entities can only own a specific interest, or type of partial ownership, in land. This historic anomaly is explained below.

Many laypeople are puzzled by the feudal origins of English land law and find it is an overly complex and illogical system. Indeed, a consumer wishing to gain basic knowledge of the leasehold system can easily be put off when glancing through the many textbooks that exist on land law in England. Several of these weighty tomes start off with a list of statutes that are relevant to land law, beginning in 1215 with the Magna Carta. The outdated terminology used in the leasehold system, including defining the owner of the flat as a 'tenant', conjures up feudal images of the lord of the manor and his chattel.

We can see why. As explained later, today's residential property system, with the landlord as freeholder and the leasehold flat owner as tenant, has origins dating back to the 'free tenures' of William the Conqueror's landholding nobles and the 'unfree tenures' of the peasant labourers known as 'villeins'.

This book aims to equip the layperson with a broad working knowledge of the leasehold system; to demystify the terminology and to explain in clear terms the best-practice solutions for avoiding common problems in owning, buying or selling leasehold property in England and Wales. Scotland and Northern Ireland, which have different property systems, are not covered in this book.

The recent increase in construction of new apartment buildings, whether designed for young professionals, senior citizens or other homeowner groups, is lending new urgency to the need for consumers to understand the leasehold system. While changes in legislation have made it possible for property developers to abandon the antiquated leasehold system entirely and to offer UK homeowners the new equivalent of the US condo, in the form of 'commonhold' ownership of a building, there are few signs of this happening. Instead, the number of new leasehold flats across the country is growing rapidly.

This book has been written for increasingly well-informed and empowered consumers who have grown tired of hearing solicitors say leasehold is too complicated a system to explain and who are exasperated by less-well-trained estate agents who claim incorrectly that it makes no difference whether a flat is leasehold or share-of-freehold or how many years are left on the lease. We also aim to deliver knowledge, literacy and information tools that will enable an increasingly large number of leaseholders of flats to enjoy their right to gain fuller ownership of their unit and building, through the process of freehold purchase.

Why does leasehold matter?

Why is the leasehold system such an enormous problem in this country? One finds other instances of out-of-date legislation. Why do the antiquated principles in England's land law deserve such special attention? The answer lies in the enormous amount of money spent each year on leasehold property by consumers across the socio-economic spectrum. The government estimates that there are 1.5 million leasehold flats in England and Wales, mostly located in London and South-East England, although industry experts say that the actual number is probably closer to four million. According to government statistics, up to one-third of leasehold flats are contained in so-called conversions: houses that were originally constructed as one-family homes, with the remainder found in purpose-built blocks. In addition, the government estimates that there are nearly one million leasehold houses, about half of which are in North-West England and the Merseyside region.

Walking past estate agents' shopfronts in various parts of London, one will see leasehold flats for sale that range in price from below £50,000 to above £2 million. Wander through Marylebone, past a 50-flat mansion block, where the average flat might be worth £500,000, and you have just walked past £25 million in real estate. In prime locations in Knightsbridge or Mayfair, the collective value of flats in such buildings tops £100 million.

But do these people truly own their homes? Do they have the level of control over their homes that enables them to protect the value of their property and to ensure that their buildings are well-maintained? The answer in most cases is no, no and no. By owning a leasehold property, a person or entity owns a lease, which is a contract with the landlord, or freeholder, that identifies the rights and responsibilities of both parties. The lease normally states that the freeholder must provide adequate maintenance of the building, including items such as cleaning and porterage, and to have necessary repairs carried out. In the lease, it is usually stated that the leaseholder is responsible for paying for all of this maintenance and repair work, in the form of a 'service charge' that is commonly levied every six or 12 months. The lease will also specify the year in which it was created and the length of the lease from the start, thus identifying the number of years left during which the buyer enjoys the right of possession and use. Other rights and responsibilities spelled out in the lease are discussed in more detail in chapter 1, 'What to look for when buying a leasehold property'.

Because the leaseholder owns an interest, or a restricted type of ownership, in the flat and because the lease is limited in time, this property is a net wasting asset, although in a rising property market its value may increase. Every year that goes by strips value from the flat. In the case of flats with over 100 years, this is not a large problem, since the expiration of the lease is so far in the future that it more closely resembles true ownership. But for flats that have 80 years or less, the wasting-asset issue becomes more apparent. By the time a lease is down to 60 or 50 years, the flat can become difficult to sell and mortgage lenders are more reluctant to provide mortgages.

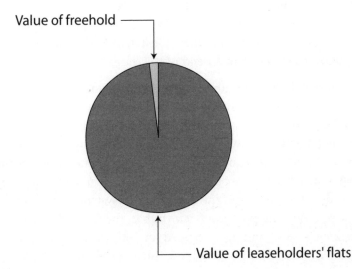

Value of freehold

Value of leaseholders' flats

The pie chart above illustrates one of the most bewildering aspects of the leasehold property system. Consider a sample building in London, a mansion block with 50 leasehold flats, each of which has an average market value of £500,000. In this case, the collective leaseholders' interest totals £25 million. That is, the residents together own an asset worth that amount. On the other hand, the freeholder, who enjoys nearly total control of the building, may own an interest with a market value of only, say, £500,000 – a mere two per cent of the total owned by the residents. This is just one example. The value of the freehold of a building depends on several factors, including the number of years left on the leases, the amount of ground rent paid and the number of residents that are seeking to buy the freehold. This is explained in detail in chapter 4, 'Calculating the freehold price'.

While the landlord holds nearly total ownership and control of the building, he bears a disproportionately small amount of the cost and risk of doing so, since it is the leaseholders that are obliged to pay for all maintenance and repairs on the structure. This long-standing imbalance in rights and responsibilities has helped to explain the existence of widespread abuse by landlords of blocks of flats, particularly up to the end of the last century. Many government-sponsored studies have been carried out on problems with the leasehold system in recent decades. These have repeatedly identified two main complaints by leaseholders. The first is that many landlords have failed to maintain buildings properly and/or have overcharged leaseholders for service charges. The second is that leaseholders, despite having sometimes invested a lot of time, money and effort in improving their flats, still suffer from the wasting-asset aspect of their leasehold property and they must hand over ownership of the property to the landlord at the end of the lease.

Since the mid-1900s a number of governments in the United Kingdom, those led by both the Conservative and the Labour Parties, and many consumer groups, have identified serious problems with the leasehold system, notably that the system grants an unfairly large amount of power to landlords, to the detriment of leaseholders. Several governments since the 1960s, including those of John Major in 1993 and Tony Blair in 2002, have made attempts to reform the leasehold system in order to address these inequities. The process of reform has, for the end-consumer, been painstakingly slow and has resulted in only limited success. This is explained in more detail in chapter 3, 'Buying the freehold'. The problem became so severe that it was not uncommon throughout the 1990s to hear leaseholders complaining of freeholders behaving virtually like 'slum landlords' by failing to maintain buildings properly, even in some of London's most prestigious residential neighbourhoods.

The outdated nature of the leasehold system has become increasingly apparent as it affects an ever larger cross-section of the population. Up through the 1980s, one often heard professionals in the UK, ranging in age from 30s up to 50s, say they avoided living in a block of flats, even architecturally elegant Edwardian mansion blocks. Many members of the middle class said they preferred to own a house, even if it were small and outside of London, in order to have their own roof and garden. These consumers said they viewed mansion blocks as the suitable destinations only for the two homeowner groups with the most limited options, that is, first-time buyers and senior citizens. They said there was a stigma attached to living in these buildings, because they were generally recognised as poorly-maintained.

But the image associated with living in a flat has changed dramatically in recent years because of shifting demographics, and changes in lifestyle and working habits. An increasingly large proportion of Britons and other residents in the United Kingdom are becoming flat owners, as competition in the workplace prompts many employees to live nearer to work and to evening leisure spots, and to cut down on commuting time. A rise in geographic mobility in the workforce also means that a growing number of Britons have lived in other countries and have brought back home a greater appreciation of the urban lifestyle, including living in a high-rise apartment building near shops, restaurants and other amenities.

There has also been growing interest in buying flats as a result of the buy-to-let trend, in which consumers become amateur landlords by buying flats as pure financial investments and letting them out. In addition, rising affluence has prompted many Britons, who would previously have sought to buy a house in a London suburb, now to splash out by buying a pied-à-terre apartment in London and a house in the countryside where they can relax at the weekend and on holiday.

Virtually every sector of the population has shown a new or growing interest in owning a flat, including the thousands of households that bought units in council housing following the then Prime Minister Margaret Thatcher's right-to-buy initiative in the 1980s, which was aimed at broadening home ownership. Since the 1990s, the government has dedicated new focus on blocks of flats as solutions for addressing London's acute and long-standing housing shortage. It is a logical step to explore ways in which to provide more housing by building up rather than out within the context of urban areas.

How did we get here?

How did we end up with such a complicated system of residential ownership? Where do the terms leasehold and freehold come from? The answers provide a fascinating journey back through English history, beginning with William the Conqueror in 1066. In fact, land law in this country as we know it today has evolved over the past ten centuries, with a surprisingly large number of concepts that have survived the test of time.

When William, the illegitimate son of the Duke of Normandy, landed at Pevensey in Sussex in 1066, his large invasion force comprised of fighting men who expected rewards if they were victorious. After William's army defeated King Harold, the Anglo-Saxon ruler, at the Battle of Hastings on 14 October 1066, the Conqueror immediately laid claim to all of the country. He was crowned King of England in Westminster Abbey on Christmas Day 1066. In one of the most sweeping land-grabs in history, William I declared that all land in England belonged to him. Indeed, this rule has never been reversed, which is why, technically speaking, all land in England still belongs to the Crown, with various types of subordinate rights to the land being assigned to various parties.

In recognition of the service rendered to William by his Norman invading force, he quickly began to distribute land to the men who had fought for him. Because there were no centralised records of who owned which land, William granted to approximately 200 of his most important Norman followers the use of manors and large tracts of land that had belonged to Anglo-Saxons who had fled or died in fighting after the invasion. William's main followers in the Norman Conquest thus quickly became the new power structure throughout the land. In 1086, when William I ordered his Royal Commissioners to carry out an extensive land survey of England, the documents they produced, later called the Domesday Book, identified the new power elite. The relatively short list of landowners in the Domesday Book revealed the most influential men in the land. In medieval times, virtually all power came from the control of land. It was the greatest source of income, military might and prestige, and was considered the only worthwhile investment.

When William granted land in England to this group of his followers, he did so in exchange for specific services that they had to provide to him in return. These new landholders became known as tenants and their landholdings were called tenures, from the Latin 'tenere', to hold. This concept laid the foundation for the feudal system of landholding. While the noblemen (women would not have been included at the time) held land of the king in exchange for a service, they in turn divided up their holdings and granted land to subordinate tenants, who owed them an identified service in return. Tenure meant that the landholder did not have absolute ownership of the land, but derived the right of possession from someone else. Through a system that became known as subinfeudation, a pyramid structure with up to eight levels of different landholdings and owed services developed. The 200-odd tenants who held land of the king were known as tenants-in-chief. As shown in the diagram below, some tenants-in-chief owed a military service to the king. According to this 'tenure in chivalry', they were obliged to provide the king with a certain number of armed men for a specific number of days each year. The king used these knights to make up a large part of his army.

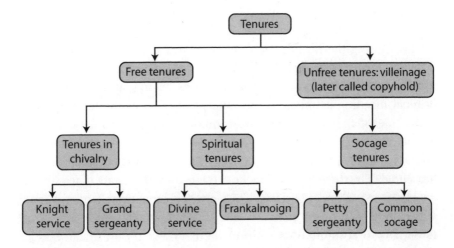

Other tenants owed services to the king that were religious in nature. According to a 'spiritual tenure', an abbey might be granted land in exchange for celebrating a certain number of special masses for the king for a particular period of time, or to spend an identified amount of time praying for his soul. 'Frankalmoign tenure' included granting lands in charity to religious bodies. Another type of landholding was 'socage tenure', which meant that the tenant held his land in return for performing certain duties for the overlord. These duties were, over the centuries, translated into payments of money. Tenures in chivalry, spiritual tenures and socage tenures were all known as 'free tenures', while the type of landholding made possible for the majority of tenants was known as 'unfree tenure'. These tenants were so-called 'villeins': the peasant labourers who carried out work for the overlord that was not specified or limited in quantity or quality. The villeins had to do the bidding of the lord of the manor. Farm land across the country was cultivated by those holding either socage tenure or villeinage.

The feudal system included a myriad of other types of services. People were granted land in exchange for feeding the animals near the king's hunting grounds, for providing the king with a meal when he hunted nearby and for carrying his banner when he visited the area. In the 12th century a man named Rolland was granted land in Suffolk in exchange for performing as a jester at court. Indeed, his lease specified in Latin that he had to perform 'unum saltum et siffletum et unum bumbulum', in other words 'a leap, a whistle and a fart', every Christmas Day for the king.

Over the centuries tenures in chivalry and spiritual tenures disappeared, while socage tenure came to represent the basis of all modern property estates. During the Middle Ages, the term 'estate' came to be applied to different forms of tenure. While 'estate' in its common modern sense usually refers to land and/or collected assets belonging to a person, the original meaning is linked to the concept of time. In the feudal period, 'estate' meant a right to enjoy possession of a piece of land for a specified period of time. During the Middle Ages, there were three types of freehold estate in land. The term 'freehold' is far more ancient a term than 'leasehold'. The three types of freehold estate were the 'estate in fee simple', 'estate in fee tail' and 'life estate'. The word 'fee' came from 'fief' and 'feud', which were both terms of feudal law. An 'estate in fee simple' amounted essentially to absolute ownership of the land and meant that the estate could be inherited by one's heirs. An 'estate in fee tail' was one that could be inherited and that could not be sold or transferred outside the identified line of succession. The medieval word 'tail' came from the French word 'tailler', to cut, since any failure by a holder in estate of fee tail to pass on the land to an heir resulted in the landholding being severed and reverting to the previous family holder or his heir. The system of 'estate in fee tail' was devised by powerful landed families to try to keep the land within the blood line and to prevent spendthrift heirs from selling off property. A 'life estate' was a landholding that lasted for the life of the tenant and that ended upon his death.

In common law, a fourth type of estate was added centuries later, the leasehold estate. From the class-defined origins of the feudal landholding system, only one type of tenure of land now remains. This is the estate in fee simple for the tenure of common socage, which is basically the equivalent of being the owner of the land.

Since 1925, there have been only two types of legal estate in land, both of which originate in the feudal system. They are 'fee simple absolute in possession', which means freehold, and 'terms of years absolute', which

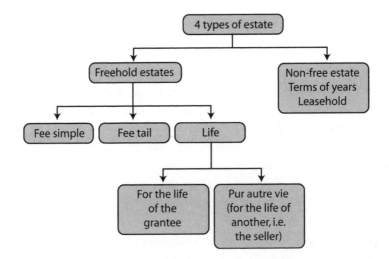

means leasehold. The word 'absolute' in this sense means to go on forever. The phrase 'terms of years' means a property holding that lasts for the number of years specified in the lease. The freehold is the greater of the two when compared to the leasehold, since the freeholder holds the land for an infinite amount of time. The modern term 'landlord' comes directly from the feudal concept of the overlord to whom the tenant owed a service in exchange for the possession and use of land.

The way forward

Moving forward in time, the United Kingdom entered the 20th century with a spaghetti-like collection of land laws. In an attempt to create order and structure from a legislative mess, and as a result of reform activity in the housing sector that had taken place behind the scenes in the 1800s, six major land laws were passed in 1925. Much of today's legislation draws from these, especially the Law of Property Act 1925. While the 1925 legislation codified the law and systemised it, it did not make fundamental changes to earlier land law.

The next events to have a major impact on regulations and conditions for flat dwellers were the two World Wars, and a series of groundbreaking laws during the inter-war period concerning the rights of renting tenants. From 1920 to 1946, about a dozen Rent Acts were passed that limited the amount by which landlords could increase rents being charged to tenants and also restricted the right of landlords to evict tenants. While this legislation was aimed at protecting renting tenants, it had the effect of virtually drying up the rental market, since the owners of blocks of flats found that they were unable to run a profitable business through renting out units. Many landlords decided, as a result, to draw capital from their property holdings by creating and selling long leases for the flats. Typically, the leases were for a term of 99 years, but some were for 125 years or a different period. By the latter part of the 20th century, a growing number of flats in urban areas such as central London were available only as so-called long leasehold properties, rather than as rentals, with 'long lease' being defined as a lease lasting for more than 21 years from the start. Many houses throughout the country were also sold as leasehold properties, with the freeholder continuing to maintain control of the land and holding the right to recover the property at the end of the lease.

In 1967, an important law was passed that gave leaseholders of houses a new right to gain near total ownership of their properties. The Leasehold Reform Act 1967 gave leaseholders of certain categories of houses the right to compel the landlord to sell them the freehold. This legislative change was the result of concern over conditions for a group of people in South Wales who lived in leasehold houses originally constructed in the 1800s by powerful landowners for labourers working in the coal mines. The 1967 Act gave the freehold-purchase right to some, not all, of the leaseholders of houses and did not cover leasehold flats. Nearly three decades later, leaseholders of flats gained the right for the first time to compel the landlord to sell them the freehold of their building and to do so at a fair market price, within a statutory timeframe. The then Prime Minister John Major was in office and his government pushed the Leasehold Reform, Housing and Urban Development Act 1993 through a somewhat unwilling Parliament. While the 1993 Act broke new ground by giving flat owners this new right of so-called 'collective enfranchisement', it contained several restrictions that made it difficult to implement. For instance, two-thirds of all leaseholders in a building had to participate in order to enfranchise and half of the participants had to pass a residence qualification which required that their flat be their only or principal home. Leaseholders that had their principal home elsewhere or that owned their flat through a company or trust were not allowed to participate.

Despite the large effort required by the Conservative government to get the 1993 Act passed, including getting it past a number of large landholding Conservative peers in the House of Lords, the law produced little immediate result. Only a small number of leaseholder groups enfranchised in the following years, mainly because of the many restrictions the law contained. Prospects for leaseholders who wanted to enfranchise improved significantly a decade later, with the passage of the Commonhold and Leasehold Reform Act 2002. This legislation removed many of the limitations contained in the 1993 Act, including the residence requirement and the ban on participation by leaseholders that were companies. Under the 2002 Act, only half of all flats in the building had to participate in order to enfranchise. The law, which is described in detail in chapter 3, 'Buying the freehold', did not solve all the problems relating to the leasehold system. The legislation remains complex and difficult to understand, and the process of enfranchising continues to be time-consuming, highly technical and unwieldy. But the 2002 Act was important in moving flat dwellers one step closer towards enjoying full ownership and control of their homes.

CHAPTER 1

What to look for when buying a leasehold property

Consumers must take care, when acquiring a leasehold property, to ensure that they are actually buying what they think they are buying. There is widespread misunderstanding about the nature of leasehold properties. This includes a mistaken impression many people have that they are buying a residential property over which they have full and everlasting ownership. As we saw in the Introduction, purchasing a leasehold property means one is buying a lease that provides a specified right to possess and inhabit the property for a finite period of time.

This chapter identifies the most important things to look for when buying a leasehold property, including understanding the main elements of the lease, identifying running costs and avoiding common pitfalls when making the purchase. Although much of the information covered in this chapter applies to both leasehold flats and leasehold houses, our main focus will be on flats.

Getting a copy of the lease

It is consumer best-practice, when considering whether to buy a leasehold property, to obtain a copy of the lease and examine it carefully before making a decision. The lease describes all the rights and obligations of the landlord and the leaseholder. Unfortunately, in too many instances, leaseholders are prepared to buy a flat without first seeing the lease. Many estate agents claim that it is too difficult for them to obtain copies of leases for every would-be buyer. Many sellers do not hold the original lease themselves, because they have asked their solicitor to keep it, or their mortgagee has it. It can also be nerve-racking, if one has set one's heart on buying a particular leasehold property and other prospective buyers are making offers, to delay the process by searching for a copy of the lease. But it is almost always worth doing. In any case, every leasehold property owner should have a copy of his lease and should be ready to provide a copy to a serious potential buyer.

If the seller does not provide a copy of the lease, it is possible to obtain a copy from HM Land Registry. This is the government body that holds the records of all land property titles. As a result of the passage of the Land Registration Act 2002, members of the public now have largely increased access to copies of freehold and leasehold title documents and leases. In the past, one had to be the owner of a property to get a copy of the lease. But this changed with the Land Registration Act 2002, which has resulted in the creation of a more modern system for handling and storing property titles. The new set up is aimed at providing greater access to the public to property ownership documents, making more efficient use of technology and the internet, and paving the way for electronic conveyancing.

If the owner of a property says that he does not have a copy of the lease or if he is slow in providing it, the prospective buyer should write to the Official Copy Deeds Section of the relevant HM Land Registry office explaining why the lease is required and enclosing the relevant Land Registry form and payment. It usually costs less than £10 to get a copy of a lease. Appendix 1, 'Useful contacts' has details of the main office of HM Land Registry.

The main elements contained in a lease

The format and wording used in leases, some written many decades ago, can vary widely and many of the old-fashioned terms used can appear indecipherable, but the would-be buyer should not be put off. The Glossary at the end of this book provides terms commonly used, such as 'demised', which means the grant of a leasehold interest, and 'demised premises', which means the flat or house that is the subject of the lease. The main elements in the lease fall into five categories: the premises demised by the lease; the rights granted and excepted; the repairs, alterations and decorations; insurance; and rent and service charges.

Premises demised: This section of the lease identifies precisely the property being leased. The lease should also contain a floor plan of the unit.

Rights granted and excepted: This section should include all rights and restrictions, including rights of access to the building and its common parts, and the right to run services such as gas or electricity through the building into the flat.

Repairs, alterations and decorations: This section identifies whether it is the landlord or the leaseholder who is responsible for carrying out repairs, alterations and decorations. In most large blocks of flats, the landlord is responsible for repairs to the building excluding those inside a leasehold flat, and for decorating the outside of the building and/or window frames after a specified number of years.

Insurance: This section identifies which party is responsible for insuring the building and describes the required extent of the insurance. It is normally the responsibility of the landlord in a large building to insure the whole structure, but in some buildings the tenants can be made jointly responsible. If the landlord is responsible, the lease will usually say the building must be insured for the full reinstatement value if the building were destroyed. Leaseholders have a right to receive a copy of the insurance policy. The cost of insuring the building is borne by the leaseholders and is included in the service charges.

Ground rent and service charges: This information is usually located in two separate sections of the lease. Ground rent and service charges, which are paid by the leaseholder, are described below.

Ground rent

Buyers often dedicate maximum focus on the sale price when trying to decide whether to buy a particular flat, but it is also essential to identify the property's ongoing costs. One running cost for a leasehold flat is the ground rent. Because leasehold is a tenancy, it is subject to a rent on the land which is paid to the freeholder. This is paid by the leaseholder in the form of ground rent. The amount of ground rent for a flat in central London can vary from a nominal amount each year, such as £50, to a few thousand pounds. The amount of ground rent payable must always be identified in the lease. In some cases, the ground rent will be set at a specific and unchanging amount. In other instances, the lease will identify the initial ground rent and increased amounts payable after specific periods of time. The leaseholder normally has to pay the ground rent on an annual basis or every six months. The landlord or the managing agent company employed by the landlord to run the building usually sends the leaseholder an invoice covering both ground rent and service charge.

Service charges

The main running cost of a leasehold flat is the so-called variable service charge. This is the amount of money that must be paid each year to the landlord to cover the leaseholder's share of the cost of managing and maintaining the building. The landlord is normally responsible for ensuring that the building is properly maintained and that necessary repairs are carried out. Service charges include the cost of cleaning, porterage, lighting and insuring the building. They can also include items such as central heating, and maintenance and repairs of a central boiler and lift. The lease identifies all the ways in which the landlord is obliged to maintain the building and lists all the items that are payable by the leaseholders in the form of service charges.

The lease should identify the percentage of total service charges for the whole building that the leaseholders must pay. In most cases, the landlord does not make any financial contribution to the service charges. The lease should specify how often the service charges are to be paid. Unless the lease states that they are to be paid in advance, they are payable in arrears. The service charge is called variable because it can vary from year to year, depending on whether building running costs have increased or decreased, and whether any major repairs or maintenance, so-called 'major works', have been carried out. A buyer should find out from the vendor the average annual amount of service charges and should also obtain a copy of the service charge summary for the past three years. The service charge for a leasehold flat in central London can vary from a few hundred pounds to several thousand, depending on the size and market value of the flat, the size of the building and the level of services provided, such as whether there is 24-hour, seven-day porterage.

By law, landlords are obliged to send a summary of service charges each year to any leaseholders that are invoiced for these charges. Flat owners have the legal right to demand such a summary and also to challenge service charges if they believe the amounts to be unreasonable. Chapter 2, 'Service charge disputes and other grounds for litigation' explains this in detail. If a vendor says that he does not receive from the landlord a summary of service charges, this is an indication for the buyer of a building that is not managed at a proper level, as required by law.

Some buildings are managed directly by a landlord, whether a company or individual, while in other cases the landlord will hire a company called a managing agent to run the building, provide the necessary services and carry out any required repairs. It is best practice in larger blocks of flats for the landlord to hire a managing agent, since this often results in greater specialisation of management service, increased transparency of fees and more accountability to the leaseholder. Whether the landlord manages the building himself or hires a managing agent to do it, it is customary that a management fee be included in the service charges. This should be made clear in the lease. The different fee structures of managing agents is described below.

When leaseholders join forces to buy the freehold of a block of flats, they often identify the share of the cost to be paid by each participant by referring to the service charge percentage in each lease. Since the service charge percentages represent the pro rata running costs being paid by leaseholders, these same percentages are often used to allocate the share of the freehold cost and the share of the new resident management company that will be owned by the participants. This is explained in more detail in chapter 3, 'Buying the freehold'.

Subletting and other restrictions

The purchase of a leasehold property can end in heartache if the buyer is mistaken in believing that he has the right to do certain things following the acquisition. This is why it is essential to get a copy of the lease before buying a leasehold property. As we have seen, a lease is a property right, since it is an estate in land. Because of this, the leaseholder has a right to assign, or transfer, the lease to someone else. Using legal jargon, this is the right of 'alienation', a term dating back to feudal times that means the voluntary transfer of an estate in land from one party to another. The leaseholder also has the right to sub-lease or sublet, which means he creates a 'subordinate' lease out of his lease. Finally, the leaseholder has a right to part with possession of the property in the form of a licence, such as allowing a friend to stay in a leasehold flat for a period of time. But it is important to check the lease carefully for possible restrictions on these and other assumed rights.

There are two types of lease that usually contain an 'absolute covenant' under which a tenant is banned from assigning, subletting or parting with possession. These are the short-term lease, which lasts for a period of a few months to a few years, and the periodic tenancy, which is for a set period of time such as a month or a year and which goes on extending until the landlord or tenant gives notice. Many business leases are periodic tenancies. Medium-term lettings, lasting from about ten to 50 years, usually contain a 'qualified covenant' under which the tenant can assign, sublet or part with possession, but only if the landlord provides consent. Long leases, such as those with a term of 99 years, normally allow the tenant to assign, sublet or part with possession, but often a written go-ahead from the landlord must first be obtained. The law says, however, that the landlord cannot unreasonably withhold this permission.

If a buyer is investing in a leasehold property with the express purpose of renting it out, it is critical that he finds out whether the landlord normally grants approval for subletting. Regarding other possible restrictions, some leases will state that there is a ban on pets or having bare, wood floors, because of the noise created for residents living in the flat below. The leases of many mansion blocks built in the late 1800s or early 1900s contain restrictive covenants on leaseholders installing double glazing on windows or carrying out other work that would alter the appearance of the exterior of the building.

One subject that causes problems for many would-be buyers is that of interior alterations. Most modern leases contain clauses that ban leaseholders from taking down, moving or erecting walls within the flat, unless prior consent from the landlord has been obtained. To gain the right to do such work, leaseholders must get permission from the landlord in the form of a deed of variation. This deed becomes part of the title documentation that must be handed over to the new leaseholder when the flat is sold. Sometimes a vendor will have difficulty selling a flat because a previous leaseholder carried out alterations on the property without getting the landlord's permission and without getting a deed of variation. In such cases, the landlord will often force the leaseholder to pay a penalty for the work carried out years earlier by a previous owner, before the landlord will sign a deed of variation that retroactively approves the work. Many leasehold property sales have been delayed for months or fallen through entirely because of issues such as this.

Sinking funds and planned future expenses

There is a growing interest amongst professionals with children to buy flats in London, especially in some of the beautiful red-brick mansion blocks built a century ago. While many such households had previously sought to move to the suburbs with the arrival of children, an increasing number are now opting for the convenience of living in an urban centre, closer to work and in a building with a porter, lift and other communal services. However, all buyers must take care to find out not only the expected annual amount of service charges that will be payable in these buildings, but also whether there are expensive repairs or renovation projects coming up and whether the building has a sinking fund to address these.

A sinking fund, also known as a reserve fund, is one into which leaseholders pay a certain amount of money each year for planned future major works. By paying a set annual amount into the fund, leaseholders are able to accumulate the resources needed without having to make sudden large expenditures in just one or two years. In a building that is run by a managing agent, it is the managing agent that holds the sinking fund on trust for the leaseholders. Unfortunately, a large number of leases for older buildings in England and Wales contain no clause or allowance for a sinking fund. In such a case, the landlord is not allowed to ask the leaseholders to create or pay into such a fund. This defect in leases has prompted many leaseholders, once they have grouped together to buy the freehold, to include a clause on sinking funds when they replace, or 'vary', the lease. We revisit the subject of sinking funds in chapter 2, 'Service charge disputes and other grounds for litigation'.

Head leaseholders

Confusion can sometimes emerge when a buyer discovers that the leasehold property purchased has more than one landlord. This is the case when the freeholder, who holds the so-called 'superior' lease on the property, sells what is called an 'intermediate' lease to a different entity. This results in three different levels of ownership in the building. The freeholder has the highest level of overall ownership. Beneath him is the so-called head leaseholder or head lessee and at the bottom is the leaseholder. It is essential, before buying a leasehold property, to identify precisely which person or company owns which interest in the building. The lease should clarify these points. One can also carry out an online search at HM Land Registry, by visiting www.landregisteronline.gov.uk, clicking on 'Property enquiry' and typing in the title number, if it is known, or the full address of the property. It is the immediate, superior landlord that is responsible to the leaseholder for managing and maintaining the building. If a building has a freeholder and a head leaseholder, then it is the head leaseholder that is directly responsible to leaseholders.

Buying in a building that is enfranchising

There has been a sharp increase in recent years in the number of leaseholders who have joined forces in order to compel their landlord to sell to them the freehold of the building, in the process known as collective enfranchisement. This process is described in detail in chapter 3, 'Buying the freehold'. Because of the growing market demand for flats in buildings that are 'share of freehold' rather than owned by absentee corporate landlords, many buyers are finding themselves making an offer for a flat in a building that has started but not yet completed this process. It is important to bear in mind that in a large building the preparation and completion of the freehold purchase can often take more than a year and it is unusual for every single leaseholder to participate.

If an estate agent says residents in a building are in the process of buying the freehold, it is essential to determine whether the property for sale is a participating flat or not. This is because participating flats can expect, once the freehold has been bought, to grant themselves 999-year leases. The terms of leases for non-participants, on the other hand, normally remain unchanged. Many buyers prefer to buy a participating rather than a non-participating flat, given the expectation of the 999-year lease, but these units will demand a premium because the longer expected lease will push up the unit's market value. If the flat for sale is a participating flat, the buyer should obtain a copy of the share certificate in the resident management company that will have been set up by the leaseholders for the purpose of buying the freehold. The buyer should also ask to speak confidentially with a director of the resident management company to try to find out the estimated cost of the freehold and the share in the cost that will be payable for the flat that is being purchased.

If residents in a building have been organising to buy the freehold, but have not yet formally started the process, the buyer should find out whether there is a residents' association and, if so, whether it has been officially recognised by the landlord. The creation of a resident management company and the organisation of plans to buy the freehold can indicate that leaseholders have been unhappy with the landlord's management of the building. When buying a flat in a troubled building, the purchaser must be sure to get written confirmation that all service charges for the leasehold property have been paid up. It is common to see leaseholders in poorly-managed buildings withholding service charges from the landlord as a type of protest. Although this can create problems and unnecessary costs for the leaseholder, as explained in chapter 2, 'Service charge disputes and other grounds for litigation', it continues to be a common practice. Unfortunately, some leaseholders who have been withholding service charges, possibly for several years, try to sell their flat without telling the buyer about the service charge arrears. If the buyer acquires the leasehold property, he will become responsible for all past service charges due.

Investigating the managing agents

One way to evaluate whether a leasehold flat will be a worthwhile investment and an enjoyable home is to find out about management arrangements in the block. Buying a property in a large block of flats that is run by an established managing agent company can represent a lower-risk investment when compared to a building that is managed directly by a landlord with a poor reputation for service. Buyers should always find out which person or entity manages the building. The Association of Residential Managing Agents (ARMA) provides a list of members nationwide, all of which have signed up to an ARMA code of conduct. ARMA's details are provided in Appendix 1, 'Useful contacts'.

Although the prospective buyer of a flat is not normally in a position to bring about a change in managing agent before purchasing a property, it is important to know about recent developments in the building management business and about best practice regarding management fees. There has been a significant turnover of managing agents in the last several years in buildings where leaseholders have bought the freehold. This is because low-quality management of a building is a key motivator, prompting many leaseholders to buy their building freehold. Management problems can include overcharging for services and failing to provide accountability and financial transparency. There has also been a notable shift in the fee structure used by managing agents. In the past, large managing agent companies nearly always charged leaseholders for their management services as a set percentage of the total service charges for the building. Now, an increasing number of managing agents are charging a flat fee per annum per unit in a building, which enables leaseholders to forecast and control running costs more effectively. The flat-fee system developed as a result of complaints from leaseholders that managing agents had a financial incentive in allowing costs of major works to skyrocket, since the higher major works' costs resulted in pushing up management fees paid by residents as part of the service charges.

Defects in leases

Because a lease is a physical legal document that lasts for the duration of the term of the lease, and since it is a difficult and complex process to change or replace a lease, one often finds older leases that contain outdated clauses and clauses that by today's standards are considered defective. One common defect is for the lease to provide for insurance that has since become inadequate. In many older leases, the landlord is not required to insure the building for the full replacement value if the building is destroyed. Another defect sometimes found is the lack of so-called 'mutual enforceability'. A clause on mutual enforceability can be found in a lease, for instance, of a flat in a maisonette in which all leaseholders are responsible for maintaining certain interior parts and/or the exterior of the building. If leaseholders bear such responsibility, then the lease must make clear that there is mutual enforceability, that the leaseholder can compel fellow leaseholders to fulfil their responsibility. Another common defect in older leases is the short term of the lease as the term approaches expiry.

Changing or replacing a lease, which is called varying the lease, can be expensive and time-consuming in the best of circumstances. For the would-be buyer of a leasehold property, getting the lease changed or replaced is normally not an immediate option. However, if a buyer identifies one or more defects in the lease when purchasing the flat, it is often possible to rectify the problems later on, once the acquisition has been completed. In the case of an insufficient building insurance provision or a problem regarding mutual enforceability, the leaseholder can often get the landlord to agree to sign a separate deed of variation which puts right the particular issue. In the case of a very short-term lease, the flat owner can rectify this either by exercising his legal right to obtain from the landlord a 90-year lease extension at a fair price or by joining with fellow leaseholders to buy the freehold of the building and later be granted 999-year leases. These two procedures are explained in detail in chapter 3, 'Buying the freehold' and in chapter 5, 'Lease extensions'.

Those buying a leasehold property are often alarmed when they discover that their name does not appear on the lease. Indeed, unless a lease was created just a few years earlier, it is also unlikely for the name of the immediate vendor to appear. This is because the lease, once it is created at the beginning of the lease's term, is not changed. As each subsequent owner sells the property to a new buyer, the original and unaltered lease document simply changes hands. Because of this, normally only the names of the freeholder and the original leaseholder appear on the lease.

CHAPTER 2

Service charge disputes and other grounds for litigation

Leaseholders in England and Wales now enjoy significant protection against being forced to pay unreasonable service charges for managing and maintaining their building. The relevant legislation, including the Landlord and Tenant Act 1985 and the Commonhold and Leasehold Reform Act 2002, also guarantees leaseholders the right to be consulted by the landlord when large repairs, i.e. 'major works', are to be carried out in the building.

The existence of this legal protection has been welcomed by homeowners, although most seem to know little of their rights in this area and few appear willing to take the required steps to challenge service charges. Indeed, embarking on the legal process that is required to challenge the amount or the nature of one's service charge remains labour-intensive and time-consuming. More importantly, the fact that leaseholders have the right to challenge past service charge bills has unfortunately led many residents to get bogged down in a distracting process that, in effect, delays or prevents them from putting in place more lasting solutions to building mismanagement.

This chapter identifies leaseholders' rights regarding service charges and describes the process of challenging these charges. It also examines the advantages and disadvantages for leaseholders of engaging in service charge disputes, as compared to the pursuit of more sustainable options such as gaining the right to manage or buying the building freehold.

Rights and obligations regarding service charges

As we saw in chapter 1, 'What to look for when buying a leasehold property', most flat owners have to pay a ground rent as well as the service charge. The ground rent covers rent of the land and the amount is defined in the lease. The amount of the service charge varies each year depending on the cost of running the building. The annual service charge for a flat in a large London block might normally average £4,000. But this can shoot up to an annual £10,000 for a period of two or three years if major works, such as a new roof, are carried out and there is no sinking fund that enables leaseholders to save up for such an expenditure. While the lease should define which items are included in the service charge and should identify which percentage of the building's total service charge is payable by the individual leaseholder, the lease will not normally quantify the amount of the variable service charge.

The reasonableness of service charges

The definition of a service charge is provided in Section 18(1) of the Landlord and Tenant Act 1985, a law that was later amended by the Commonhold and Leasehold Reform Act 2002. It says that a service charge is an amount payable by a tenant 'for services, repairs, maintenance, improvements or insurance or the landlord's costs of management' and that all or part of this charge may vary as costs go up or down over time. The law says that a landlord can only charge a leaseholder a so-called reasonable amount of service charge. However, there is no definition by law of what is 'reasonable'. The landlord is also obliged to follow certain procedures when requesting that leaseholders pay their service charges and he must make available upon request documentation to back up service charge invoices.

Statements of account

Any demand by a landlord for payment of service charges must be sent to the leaseholder in writing. The landlord must also request payment for service charges within 18 months of him incurring the cost. If he does not do so within the 18 months, the landlord is not able to recover these costs, unless he advises the leaseholder in writing during the 18 months that certain costs have been incurred and that the leaseholder will be charged for these at a later date.

Under Section 21 of the Landlord and Tenant Act 1985, the leaseholder has a legal right to seek a summary of the service charge account, if the landlord has not already sent this. Any request for such a summary must be sent in writing to the landlord, or, if the landlord has hired a managing agent to run the building, to the managing agent. There is no specific form to use. The leaseholder should ask in the letter for 'a summary of the relevant costs regarding the service charges payable' for the past 12 months or the most recent financial year. The landlord, upon receiving such a written request, must send the summary of service charges to the leaseholder within one month or within six months of the end of the relevant financial year, whichever date is later.

The 2002 Act placed a greater obligation on the landlord than had previously existed regarding service charge summaries. The Act says landlords must automatically send a summary of service charges to all leaseholders that have to pay these charges, regardless of whether a summary has been requested. However, the secondary legislation that was required in order to make this particular part of the law enforceable was not expected to be created for some four years following the passage of the 2002 Act.

Once the leaseholder has received a summary of the service charges, he also has a right to require that the landlord provide back-up documentation. The leaseholder is allowed to write to the landlord within six months of receiving the service charge summary, to request access to inspect the accounts, receipts and other relevant documents regarding the charges. The landlord must by law provide this access at the relevant office within 21 days of receiving the written request.

Consultation on major works

Leaseholders have a right to be consulted formally if and when the landlord proposes to carry out repairs, renovation or other works in or on the building that will cost each service charge payer more than £250. By carrying out this consultation, the landlord also serves notice on the leaseholders that the work is planned. The landlord must serve a written notice on each leaseholder and to the secretary of any officially-recognised residents' association that describes the work to be done, explains why the work is necessary, identifies the people or companies that have been asked to submit cost quotations and that invites the leaseholders to send comments and to nominate a person or company from whom the landlord should obtain a quotation. An explanation of the meaning of an officially-recognised residents' association is provided in chapter 9, 'Residents' associations and resident management companies'. Within 30 days of receiving the landlord's notice, the leaseholders must send to him any written views or nominations for contractors.

The landlord must try to obtain cost estimates from the person or company that receives the most nominations. The next step is for the landlord to serve a second notice on the leaseholders. This notice of proposals must provide details of the work to be done and cost estimates. At least one of the contractors whose cost estimate is quoted must be unconnected with the landlord, that is, the contractor cannot be a subsidiary or associated company of the landlord. Leaseholders have a maximum of 30 days to send written observations to the landlord about this notice of proposals.

By law, the landlord must 'have regard to' any observations made by leaseholders, although this does not mean that the landlord must follow any and all recommendations made. If a leaseholder or officially-recognised residents' association has nominated an alternative contractor, the landlord must serve a notice on leaseholders once he has entered into a contract, to explain why the particular contractor was chosen. If the landlord fails to carry out the above consultation, then he will not be able to recover more than £250 from each leaseholder for the relevant work done.

If there is urgent repair work to be done in a building, such as repairing a leaking roof, the landlord can apply to the Leasehold Valuation Tribunal (LVT) to request an order to dispense with the normal consultation process. The LVT is part of the Residential Property Tribunal Service, an important quasi-judicial body which we will discuss below.

Consultation on long-term contracts

Leaseholders must be consulted when the landlord is proposing entering into a contract that will involve providing a service to the building for a period of more than 12 months and that will cost each service charge payer £100 per year or more. This could include, for instance, a contract for cleaning or gardening, or the maintenance of a lift or video intercom system. Employment contracts, such as porters' job contracts, are exempt from this consultation process.

The consultation process for long-term contracts is similar to that required for major works. The landlord must serve a notice of intention on leaseholders that informs them and invites their comments. Later the landlord must serve a further notice advising which contractor was selected. Leaseholders must send in any comments or nominations for contractors within the same time periods that apply for major works consultations.

If the landlord does not carry out the consultation on the long-term contracts as described above, he will be unable to recover more than £100 per leaseholder per year for the service provided.

Insurance

Leaseholders have the right to require that the landlord supply them with details of the insurance policy covering the building. This is the policy that insures the entire structure and is different from the contents insurance that leaseholders may have for their individual flats. A leaseholder seeking information on the insurance must send a written request to the landlord. The landlord must reply within 21 days of receipt of such a request. If the landlord has been asked for a summary of the insurance policy, this summary must include the name of the insurer, the cost of the insurance and the risks covered in the policy. The landlord is not obliged to send such a summary to a leaseholder more than once in each insurance period, which is usually one year.

Leaseholders may also require that the landlord provide 'sight of the policy', which means that he must arrange for access at the relevant office for inspection of the policy and the relevant documents, including proof of payment. The landlord can also be required to send a copy of the policy, although he has the right to charge a reasonable fee for this.

If leaseholders feel that the amount of money being charged for insurance is unreasonable, they have the right to challenge these charges at the LVT. This is discussed below.

Some leases for houses state that the leaseholder must insure the property with an insurer nominated by the landlord. The 2002 Act essentially did away with this requirement, although the secondary legislation that was required in order to make this part of the law take effect was not passed immediately after passage of the Act. Once this secondary legislation is passed, the leaseholder of a house will have the right to select his own insurer, as long as the insurer operates within the requirements of the Financial Services and Markets Act 2000.

Sinking funds

Many buildings that operate under leases dating back to the mid-1900s operate on the inefficient basis of charging leaseholders for any major works that are done, when they are done. As we saw above, this can result in a leaseholder paying, for instance, an annual £4,000 in service charges within five years of buying the flat, only to be hit by a staggering £10,000 bill in the sixth and seventh years when major works are done. The remedy for this type of spiky cost is to smooth out leaseholders' annual payments by creating a sinking fund or reserve fund. This is used to save up money over a period of several years, in order then to spend it on major works when needed. In order for a sinking fund to be created, the lease must allow for this. Many older leases have no clause or provision for a sinking fund.

When a landlord collects money from leaseholders for a sinking fund, he is essentially holding this money and the interest that it earns on trust for the leaseholders. The law says that sinking fund money must be held in a trust account for the building that is separate from the account in which regular service charges are held. If and when the building freehold is sold, the money in the sinking fund must be returned to the leaseholders.

Disputing service charges

Since the late 1990s, there have been more than 100 formal service charge disputes in England per year, with a total of 1,038 such disputes adjudicated by the Leasehold Valuation Tribunal during the period from 1999 until the end of 2004. Many of these cases were based on applications filed at the LVT by leaseholders who were challenging the reasonableness of service charges. Others were filed by landlords, who also have the right to ask the LVT to confirm whether certain service charges that have been or will be invoiced to leaseholders are reasonable. The chart below shows the number of decisions reached by the LVT on service charge disputes in recent years, including a sharp rise in 2004 as a growing number of leaseholders have learned of their right to contest these charges.

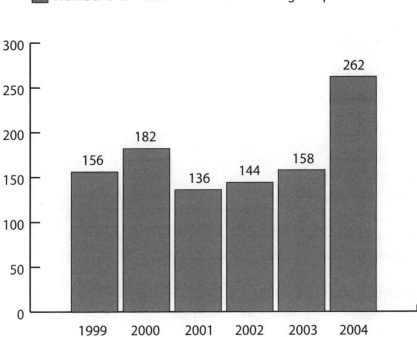

Number of LVT decisions in service charge disputes

Source of data: Residential Property Tribunal Service

While some applications filed by leaseholders at the LVT dispute service charges of less than £100, many challenge charges totalling several thousand pounds.

The process

Leaseholders wishing to challenge the reasonableness of service charges need to complete an Application Form S27A Landlord and Tenant Act 1985. This form can be downloaded from the website of the Residential

Property Tribunal Service at www.rpts.gov.uk. The RPTS, which has a special mandate to settle disputes between landlords and tenants about service charges and other issues, has five regional LVTs in England. In order to complete the seven-page S27A Form, the leaseholder or leaseholder group must identify the building, the landlord and the service charges being challenged. The completed form, a copy of the lease and a cheque in payment of the application fee must then be sent to the nearest LVT or Rent Assessment Panel. The Rent Assessment Panel is another part of the RPTS. The amount of the application fee depends on the amount of service charges being challenged. The table below shows the sliding scale for current fee amounts:

Amount of service charges in dispute	Application fee
Not more than £500	£50
More than £500 but less than £1,000	£70
More than £1,000 but less than £5,000	£100
More than £5,000 but less than £15,000	£200
More than £15,000	£350

The LVT panels that consider service charge disputes usually comprise three members: a lawyer, a valuer and a layperson. There are three possible tracks by which a service charge dispute can be handled by the LVT. In completing the S27A Form, the applicant is asked to identify which track is considered most suitable. The three tracks, from the simplest and fastest to the slowest and most complex, are:

• on paper, without a hearing;

• fast track, with a hearing;

• standard track, with a hearing and possibly a pre-trial review.

If a case is handled 'on paper', the LVT panel will receive written evidence from each party and will then reach its decision without holding an LVT hearing. The 'fast track' and 'standard track' procedures require an LVT hearing and the applicant must pay a £150 hearing fee for this. A case can be considered on the fast track if it is simple and is not expected to generate much paperwork or argument. The LVT says that it tries to hold fast track hearings within ten weeks of receiving the initial application. The standard track is for more complicated cases, including those in which several issues need to be decided and/or a lot of documentation will be required. With standard track cases, both parties may be invited to a pre-trial review, a kind of mini-hearing, so that the LVT can decide on the next steps that need to be taken before the final hearing. Standard track cases often take several months from start to finish.

Representation at the LVT hearing

Landlords that are large companies will often be represented by a solicitor at an LVT hearing regarding service charges. Smaller landlords might be represented by a managing agent or estate agent that is responsible for managing the property in question. It is not necessary, however, for either party to be represented by a solicitor or other professional advisor. Leaseholders often represent themselves. Indeed, it is difficult to find qualified, cost-effective lawyers that will represent leaseholders in service charge disputes, since these disputes can be very paper-intensive, while sometimes focusing on relatively small amounts of money.

Which court?

As we have seen, if a leaseholder wishes to challenge the reasonableness of service charges, then he must do this by filing an application with the LVT. Similarly, if the landlord wishes for an official determination to be made that service charges are reasonable, this must also be done at the LVT. If either party feels that the LVT has been wrong in reaching a decision on service charges, it is possible to appeal to a higher-level body called the Lands Tribunal. However, this can only be done if the party obtains prior approval from the LVT or the Lands Tribunal to pursue such an appeal.

The requirement to obtain this approval was put in place after leaseholders spent years complaining that landlords were abusing the system by appealing a large number of cases, even though the LVT decisions had been deemed by leaseholders and other observers to be fair.

In some cases, a service charge dispute will effectively be moved from the LVT to the County court. One such instance is explained in the section below. If one of the parties involved in a County court case wishes to appeal, this can be done in the Court of Appeal. In some cases, a dispute can go all the way up to the High Court, although this is unusual for service charge disputes.

Information on the Lands Tribunal can be found at www.landstribunal. gov.uk. Information on County courts, the Court of Appeal and the High Court is located at www.hmcourts-service.gov.uk.

To pay or not to pay?

When leaseholders in a building decide to challenge the reasonableness of service charges at the LVT, they are entitled to dispute those charges that have already been paid and/or those that have not yet been paid. When leaseholders are distressed about poor management in their building, disagreements sometimes emerge as to whether it is better to pay the service charges or withhold payment in a type of 'rent strike'. While disgruntled leaseholders may feel that withholding service charges enables them to gain some justice, this route can lead to other more serious problems.

It is important to remember that the lease is a legal contract that requires both the landlord and the leaseholder to fulfil certain obligations. This contract says that the leaseholder must pay service charges due. It also says that the landlord must maintain and manage the building. If a leaseholder believes that the landlord has failed in his contractual obligation to maintain and manage the building properly, this does not invalidate the other clauses of the lease, including the leaseholder's obligation to pay the service charges. However, if a leaseholder has filed an application with the LVT that challenges the reasonableness of the service charges, then the landlord is not allowed to begin forfeiture proceedings against him for lack of payment until after the LVT has reached a decision.

If a leaseholders' group files an application at the LVT regarding service charges that they have not paid and if the LVT decides in their favour, then they will automatically be forgiven these charges and the charges will not be paid to the landlord. If, however, the residents' group has already paid the disputed charges and they win at the LVT, then, in order to recover the charges, technically they need to file a claim in the County court to get the court to order the landlord to reimburse the charges to the residents. This is because the LVT, as a quasi-judicial body, has no legal power of enforcement in this area.

It was not always the case that leaseholders had the right to challenge the reasonableness of service charges that they had already paid. This right was enshrined in law only recently, in the Commonhold and Leasehold Reform Act 2002. Before that, some landlords had argued that leaseholders should not be able to challenge service charges which they had already paid. Years ago a leaseholder application was made to the LVT against Daejan Properties Limited, a large residential landlord, owned by the Freshwater Group of Companies, in which service charges dating back to 1989 were alleged to be excessive. The LVT found in favour of the leaseholder, saying that leaseholders could challenge charges dating back 12 years. Daejan appealed, saying it wanted a judicial review of the decision. At the appeal, the court upheld the LVT's decision. But Daejan then appealed again, this time to the Court of Appeal. In an important decision on 12 July 2001 in Daejan Properties Limited versus London LVT, the Court of Appeal found in favour of the landlord. The court overturned the lower court's and the LVT's earlier decisions and said that the leaseholders could only challenge at the LVT those service charges that had not yet been paid. The Court of Appeal said a leaseholder wishing to challenge the reasonableness of service charges already paid had to do so in the County court. This restriction on residents was abolished, however, with the Commonhold and Leasehold Reform Act 2002, which said leaseholders could challenge service charges at the LVT, whether or not these had been paid.

Leaseholders considered it progress when the 2002 Act declared that they could challenge service charges at the LVT, whether or not the charges had already been paid. But those challenging charges already paid still have to file a separate claim in the County court, to get the court to order the landlord to respect the LVT decision and reimburse the leaseholders.

The extra required step of having to file a claim in the County court means more work for residents and usually means incurring solicitors' fees. Because of this, some disgruntled leaseholders will argue in favour of the rent strike option, that is, for participating residents to refuse to pay their service charges until the LVT has reached a decision. However, it is often difficult to get a large group of residents to maintain this type of rent strike for a sustained period of time. This is because many landlords send repeated demands for payment and threaten to take legal action, which can be distracting and worrying for the recipient. Also, in large blocks of flats in urban centres such as London, people move in and out, and flat owners need to have all service charges paid up when they are seeking to sell their flat. As a result, a large committed group of angry leaseholders in year one of a rent strike campaign can easily dwindle to a small handful by year three.

If leaseholders do decide to withhold their service charges while they are filing an application with the LVT, they are advised always to pay their ground rent. As we have seen, the ground rent may be less than £50 per year, but leaseholders have a clear obligation in the lease to pay this on time. If a leaseholder fails to pay his ground rent, it is much easier for a landlord to argue that this covenant or clause in the lease has been violated and this can pave the way for the landlord to begin forfeiture proceedings.

Disputing service charges versus other options

The fact that leaseholders have the legal right to challenge the reasonableness of service charges makes some residents think this is necessarily the best option. However, a growing number of flat owners are deciding that other newly-won legal rights are more likely to deliver lasting solutions in their buildings and to cause less delay and distraction for residents. The most common problems in buildings, as identified by leaseholders, are:

- poor management, such as inadequate services, failure to carry out repairs, insufficient building security, overcharging for service charges; and
- short leases.

Poor management in the building and short leases are problems that hurt the value of a leasehold property. The main routes by which leaseholders seek to resolve one or both of these problems are:

- disputing service charges;
- getting a lease extension;
- gaining the right to manage; and

- buying the building freehold.

The ways in which leaseholders can get a lease extension, gain the right to manage or buy the building freehold are described in the next chapters.

When deciding on which route to follow, it is important to remember that few residents' associations achieve important simultaneous victories in more than one of these areas. This is because residents' associations, by their nature, are informal organisations whose leaders have little if any real authority, and because it is so easy for consensus to dwindle as leaseholders become discouraged or move away. The special organisational challenges facing the residents' association are examined in chapter 9, 'Residents' associations and resident management companies'.

When deciding what to do, residents need to analyse the degree to which each route will address past problems, such as old service charge disputes, or put in place structures and systems to address future issues. The table below helps to illustrate why an increasingly large number of leaseholders avoid embarking on time-consuming service charge disputes and choose instead to pursue a solution that will have a lasting impact on the building and on leaseholders' rights.

Leaseholder options	Resolving past problems	Addressing future issues
Disputing service charges	✔	
Getting a lease extension		✔
Gaining the right to manage		✔
Buying the freehold		✔

Finally, since some of the above options resolve more than one issue, leaseholders can often address a number of problems by pursuing a single-focused strategy. For instance, buying the freehold automatically brings with it the right to manage the building and to grant 999-year leases, and it also creates the potential to eliminate the type of poor building management that results in service charge disputes. These choices will be examined in chapters 3, 5 and 6.

Leaseholders should carefully weigh the expected costs and benefits before pursuing a service charge dispute. Some leaseholders file applications with the LVT in hopes of getting large amounts of service charges eliminated from their invoices, only to walk away disappointed when none or just a small proportion of the disputed charge is declared unreasonable by the Tribunal. In some large blocks of flats that have long been troubled by mismanagement, an obsession by a small minority of leaseholders to fight the landlord to the bitter end has resulted in years of distraction and delay before a majority of residents finally focus on buying the freehold and simply getting rid of the landlord.

Residents must avoid assuming that landlords will allow service charges to go unpaid. Many flat owners have been shocked when served with a notice that the landlord has started forfeiture proceedings over non-payment of service charges and/or ground rent. There have been numerous cases of leaseholders having to pay tens of thousands of pounds in past-due service charges in order not to lose their flats, following long but poorly-planned campaigns to fight the landlord.

CHAPTER 3

Buying the freehold

Recent changes in legislation have made it easier for leaseholders of flats to buy their building freehold, by introducing the right to compel the landlord to sell, and to do so at a fair price. The law that created this right of collective enfranchisement for flats in 1993 was significantly widened in 2002, and since then, there has been a sharp rise in enfranchisements. However, the legislation is complex and the process has been pursued by only a small minority of apartment owners. This chapter describes how a building and a resident can qualify to enfranchise and provides a step-by-step overview of the process. It also identifies the main pitfalls to avoid when buying the freehold of one's building and analyses the comparative benefits of enfranchisement versus other options that leaseholders face. Information about the other legal form in which residents of flats in England and Wales can now collectively own their building, 'commonhold', is provided at the end of the chapter.

Collective enfranchisement

In 1967, leaseholders of houses in England and Wales gained the legal right to compel their landlord to sell to them the freehold of their house and to do so for a fair price and within a statutory timeframe. The law that created this right was the Leasehold Reform Act 1967, which was later amended.

In 1993, leaseholders of flats gained the right to enfranchise by joining together to buy the freehold of their building. However, the Leasehold

Reform, Housing and Urban Development Act 1993, known as the 1993 Act, contained several restrictions that resulted in few residents seeking to enfranchise. Nine years later the right for flat owners to enfranchise was expanded with the Commonhold and Leasehold Reform Act 2002. While the 1993 Act had required that two-thirds of all leaseholders in a building participate, the 2002 Act reduced the minimum to one-half of all flats in the building. The 2002 Act also removed an earlier restriction on participation by so-called absentee leaseholders, i.e. those that did not live full-time in the building, and removed a restriction on participation by leaseholders that were companies. Since the passage of the 2002 Act, there has been a large increase in the number of leaseholders seeking to enfranchise.

As shown in the bar chart below, there were 861 applications made in 2000 to the Leasehold Valuation Tribunal (LVT) for building enfranchisements and lease extensions, but by 2004 this number had nearly trebled to 2,330.

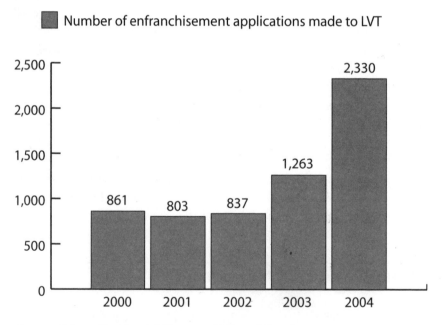

Source of data: Residential Property Tribunal Service

For reasons that are explained in chapter 5, 'Lease extensions', lease extension applications are counted in the above data along with applications for enfranchisements of residential buildings, since the former are considered to be 'individual enfranchisements'.

Qualifying to enfranchise

Not every building qualifies for collective enfranchisement. In a building that qualifies, not every tenant in the building may qualify. It is important to ensure from the start that the building and all would-be participants are eligible for enfranchisement.

The building qualification for enfranchisement

A building will be eligible for collective enfranchisement if:

1. it is a self-contained separate structure (this can include a building that is adjacent to and physically joined to another building, but that shares no common parts or common structural services with the adjacent building);

2. it has two or more flats;

3. at least two-thirds of all flats in the building are held by 'qualifying tenants', that is, tenants whose leases had more than 21 years when the leases were first granted;

4. not more than 25 per cent of the building floor space is for commercial use;

5. a minimum of half of all the flats in the building are participating, regardless of whether all the flats are leasehold or some are owned by the freeholder (if there are only two flats in a building, then both flats must participate);

6. the landlord is not a charitable housing trust or the Crown;

7. it is not a converted property of four or fewer flats, with the same person having owned the freehold since before the conversion and the freeholder or an adult member of the freeholder's family having lived in one of the flats as his only or main home for the last 12 months.

There are a few other exemptions regarding building qualification. If a leaseholder is in doubt, he should contact the Leasehold Advisory Service. Contact details are contained in Appendix 1, 'Useful contacts'.

The resident qualification for enfranchisement

A resident will qualify for collective enfranchisement if:

1. he has a 'long lease', that is, the lease term was for more than 21 years at the time it was granted; and

2. he does not own more than two qualifying flats in the building.

The main phases of collective enfranchisement

There are five phases in the formal enfranchisement process, although it should be noted that a large majority of enfranchisement initiatives are concluded with a negotiated settlement and do not proceed all the way to a hearing at the LVT. In addition to the five phases, there is important preparatory work that must be done before the official process can begin. All of the phases are described below.

The preparatory stage

When leaseholders are preparing to enfranchise a building, a minimum of 50 per cent of all flats must participate. It is best practice for the organising group to send a written notice to all leaseholders, inviting each to join in the enfranchisement and requiring a deposit upon sign-up. Before doing this, the organisers need to draw up a full list of leaseholders in the building, a task that can be speeded up by paying £2 online to get the proprietor register document for each flat from HM Land Registry. Contact details of HM Land Registry are provided in Appendix 1, 'Useful contacts'.

Once the organisers have the required number of participants and are ready to move forward, they need to create or identify a so-called 'nominee purchaser'. This is the person or entity that will buy the freehold on behalf of the participants. The Commonhold and Leasehold Reform Act 2002 does not specify how the nominee purchaser is to be chosen nor which type of legal entity is allowed. The nominee purchaser can be an individual, more than one person, a limited company or a company limited by guarantee. At present, best practice is for the nominee purchaser to be a limited company. The participants in the enfranchisement become the shareholders, and thus owners, of this nominee purchaser company. It is advisable to set up this limited company from the start as a so-called resident management company or RMC. An RMC is a company that is owned by residents who in turn own their building. Information on running an RMC is provided in chapter 9, 'Residents' associations and resident management companies'.

When the enfranchisement organisers have set up the limited company, they also need to instruct a solicitor and a surveyor, or else a professional project manager who will do this on the organisers' behalf. The surveyor needs to be instructed to carry out a confidential valuation of the freehold for the purpose of the enfranchisement. The organisers need to instruct the solicitor to draw up two legally-binding documents, the enfranchisement notice and the participation agreement. The enfranchisement notice informs the landlord that the residents are enfranchising and it advises the offered purchase price. Enfranchisers must, by law, serve an enfranchisement notice on the landlord, and they each must personally sign the document. If a participating flat is owned by three people living on three continents, each individual must still personally sign the notice. The notice cannot be signed by a leaseholder's lawyer, proxy or other representative. If a participating flat is owned by a company, the company secretary or an authorised company director must sign. A sample notice, which is also called a Section 13 Notice, is provided in Appendix 3, 'Enfranchisement notice'.

The participation agreement is a document only for the participating leaseholders and is not shown to the landlord. It is not required by law, but it is highly recommended and follows best practice. The participation agreement legally binds the participants into a consortium for the purpose of buying the freehold. It obliges each to pay his share of the freehold cost, and also, if selling a participating flat before the enfranchisement is completed, to sell to a buyer that will take the place of the vendor in the enfranchisement process. The participation agreement also needs to be signed by every participant. Appendix 4, 'Participation agreement', provides a sample.

Phase 1: The enfranchisement notice

The formal enfranchisement process begins when the enfranchisement notice is served on the landlord. This is normally served by the enfranchisers' solicitor. At this point the clock starts ticking regarding the strict deadlines established by the enfranchisement legislation. By law, the landlord has a maximum of two months by which he must reply to the notice by sending to the nominee purchaser a counter-notice. The enfranchisement notice must state the deadline date. If the landlord fails to meet this deadline, the nominee purchaser is able to buy the freehold at the offer price contained in the enfranchisement notice. It is unusual for large corporate landlords to miss the deadline.

Once the leaseholders have served the enfranchisement notice, the freeholder has the right to determine whether the participants qualify for enfranchisement by inspecting their original leases. This is called 'deducing title'. The landlord is allowed to demand access to these documents by giving as little as ten days' written notice. He also has the right to inspect the participants' flats for the purpose of carrying out a valuation. Again, he can demand this access by providing a minimum of ten days' notice. To prepare for either eventuality, enfranchisers should ensure that all participants' original leases are sent to the solicitor and possible visits to the flats by the landlord have been cleared well before the enfranchisement notice is served.

After the nominee purchaser has served the enfranchisement notice on the landlord, it must inform HM Land Registry in writing about this. This is in order to protect leaseholders against the possibility that the landlord will seek to sell the freehold to another entity. The registration with HM Land Registry is normally carried out by the enfranchisers' solicitor.

It is important to note that a minimum of 50 per cent of all flats in the building must participate at the time the enfranchisement notice is served, but this number can subsequently diminish without invalidating the notice or disqualifying the enfranchisers.

Phase 2: The landlord's counter-notice

Phase 2 begins with a counter-notice being served by the landlord on the nominee purchaser company. In the counter-notice, the landlord must:

1. acknowledge that the participants have the right to enfranchise and agree with the offer price; or

2. acknowledge that the participants have the right to enfranchisement, but state a counter-offer price; or

3. challenge the right of the participants to enfranchise.

Many landlords choose option 2, acknowledging the leaseholders' right to enfranchise, but disagreeing with the offer price. If the landlord chooses option 1, the nominee purchaser may purchase the freehold at the offer price contained in the enfranchisement notice. With option 3, the landlord must state on which grounds the enfranchisers allegedly do not qualify. The enfranchisers then have the right to challenge this, but they must do so within two months of the date of the counter-notice. In practice, the landlord challenges the validity of an enfranchisement notice by filing a claim in the County court, a process we will examine later.

Once the landlord has served the counter-notice, if it contains a counter-offer price, then the nominee purchaser and the landlord can begin negotiations and agree the terms of the freehold sale. However, they must conclude a contract of sale within two months of the date on which the terms of the sale are agreed. If they do not agree on the terms of the sale, then either side can apply to the LVT to decide the price. It is usually the nominee purchaser, rather than the landlord, that applies to the LVT.

Phase 3: The application to the LVT

Phase 3 of the enfranchisement process begins when the nominee purchaser files an application with the nearest LVT. The nominee purchaser may make the application no sooner than two months and no later than six months after the counter-notice. The nominee purchaser normally applies to the LVT through its solicitor.

Phase 4: The LVT hearing and decision

Phase 4 begins with the LVT hearing, which usually takes place three to four months from the time of application. An LVT hearing for an enfranchisement often takes one day, but it can last two. There is no official requirement for either party to be represented, but it is common practice for the nominee purchaser and the landlord each to be represented by a lawyer and a surveyor. In hotly-contested enfranchisements of large London blocks of flats, where freehold values can run into six figures, each party normally has a solicitor, a barrister and a surveyor at the LVT hearing. The LVT panel, usually comprising a lawyer, a valuer and a layperson, hears arguments from both sides regarding the proposed purchase price. It later reaches its determination and sends the written decision to both parties. The decision contains the purchase price at which the landlord is ordered to sell the freehold to the nominee purchaser.

If the nominee purchaser wishes to proceed, then it begins the process of buying the freehold. However, if the nominee purchaser does not wish to buy the freehold at the price stated by the LVT, the nominee purchaser may withdraw. The nominee purchaser is not obliged to buy the freehold at the stated price.

Phase 5: The completion of the freehold purchase

Once the LVT has sent its written decision containing the price at which the landlord must sell the freehold, the landlord must prepare a contract of sale and must give this to the nominee purchaser within 21 days of an LVT decision or within 21 days of the agreement with the nominee purchaser. The landlord may require that a ten per cent deposit be paid at the time that the contract of sale is provided. As part of the freehold purchase process, the nominee purchaser must arrange to have all the leases in the building redone, since the building will now have a new freeholder. This is referred to as 'varying' the leases.

The timeframe of enfranchisement

After the 1993 Act was passed, it took many enfranchisement initiatives years to be completed. But since 2002 the process has speeded up as a result of more rapid case handling by the LVT. The table below presents a best-case timeframe, if an enfranchising group of leaseholders moves from one phase of the project to the next at the earliest opportunity allowed by the legislation.

Event	Month in which the event occurs
The enfranchisement notice is served on the landlord by the nominee purchaser	Month 1

The counter-notice is served on the nominee purchaser by the landlord	Month 3
The nominee purchaser applies to the LVT	Month 5
The LVT hearing is held	Month 8
The LVT decision is issued	Month 9

As shown above, enfranchisers can potentially buy the freehold within a year of beginning the formal process. It should be noted, however, that the preparatory work can take many months to complete, especially if some of the participants live overseas. Also, because of the collective nature of the enfranchisement initiative, the project can only move forward during the preparatory phase as quickly as the slowest of the participants.

The costs of buying the freehold

Leaseholders can sometimes focus all their attention on what they expect the freehold to cost, without taking into consideration other required expenditures. The main costs in buying the freehold of one's building are:

- the share of the freehold;

- stamp duty on the freehold cost;

- solicitors' fees;

- surveyors' fees; and

- administrative costs, which may include setting up a limited company, hiring a company secretary and hiring accountants.

The costs excluding the LVT

Enfranchisers are liable not only for their own solicitors' and surveyors' fees, but also for the landlord's so-called reasonable solicitor and surveyor fees up to and excluding an LVT hearing. This is because the law says the landlord, when faced with this type of compulsory sale, should have his costs covered when dealing with the enfranchisement notice, including the confirmation that the leaseholders qualify to enfranchise. The landlord also has his costs covered for inspecting the participating flats and carrying out his own valuation. The law does not quantify what is 'reasonable'. But if enfranchisers feel that they are being charged unreasonably at the end of the enfranchisement process, they can challenge the amount at the LVT.

If enfranchisers withdraw their enfranchisement notice at any stage before an LVT hearing or if there is a deemed withdrawal, then the nominee purchaser is liable for the landlord's reasonable costs up to that stage.

The costs at the LVT

When leaseholders apply, through their nominee purchaser, to the LVT for an enfranchisement, there is no application fee.

Enfranchisers are not liable for the landlord's costs at an LVT hearing. In preparing for an LVT hearing and in appearing at a hearing, each side pays its own costs, including when a solicitor, barrister and/or surveyor is instructed. Leaseholders are not required to be represented by a solicitor, barrister and surveyor, but large blocks of flats do normally have this level of representation. The fact that landlords have to pay their own way if a case goes all the way to an LVT hearing explains why so many landlords reach negotiated settlements with nominee purchasers just before a scheduled LVT hearing takes place.

Many solicitors and surveyors specialising in enfranchisement charge an hourly fee. While some will provide an estimate regarding the number of hours needed to to do the required work for an enfranchisement, a surprisingly-large number refuse to do so. Rates for solicitors in London that specialise in enfranchisement range from about £150 to over £400 per hour. In some cases, however, leaseholders are able to get a flat-fee quotation from these professional advisors or from the small number of project management firms that work for enfranchisers.

The success factors in enfranchisement

This section identifies important issues that come up during enfranchisements and presents solutions for avoiding some of the main potential pitfalls. Several of these issues are also addressed in case study B in Appendix 2, 'Case studies'.

Non-participants

Many enfranchisement efforts unravel within the first months of preparation because too great an emphasis is placed on getting every leaseholder to sign up. It is important to remember that unanimity is not required and, in a large building, is rarely obtained. Remember, a minimum of only 50 per cent of all flats in a building need to participate in order for the leaseholders to enfranchise. While all qualifying leaseholders should be invited to join, organisers should not allow a small number of opponents or fence-sitters to hold up or derail the process.

The organisers can minimise the likelihood of conflict and tension developing amongst residents during or after an enfranchisement by being clear from the start that participants will be able to get 999-year leases at a nominal fee, such as £1 plus legal costs, after the freehold purchase, while non-participants will not enjoy this right. Enfranchisements proceed most smoothly when written notices that are sent to leaseholders to invite them to join the enfranchisement have a clearly identified opening date, closing date and an indication of the expected costs for participants. In large buildings, the sign-up period can last a few weeks or several months. The notification in writing of a non-negotiable closing date of the invitation to participate decreases the likelihood of confusion and makes it difficult for latecomers to claim that they did not know that there was a sign-up deadline.

Once an enfranchisement notice has been served on a landlord, the participants must treat the process as strictly confidential and not discuss it with non-participants living in the building or elsewhere. There are two particularly important reasons for this. The first is that some large landlords have been known to try to glean information about an enfranchisement initiative, including valuation report details, from non-participating residents in the building. Secondly, a landlord has a right to declare an enfranchisement notice invalid if he can prove that enfranchisement participants have discussed with non-participating residents prices or other terms at which the non-participants might be sold lease extensions and/or a share in the freehold after the process has been completed. If enfranchisers do invite a non-participant into the enfranchisement process after the initial notice has been served on the landlord, they must inform the landlord of this in writing, and must also revise their offer price and the enfranchisement notice accordingly.

Leasebacks

If leaseholders are enfranchising a building that contains both leasehold flats and flats owned by the landlord, they must be familiar with the principle of so-called 'leaseback'. By law, a landlord has the right to keep control of any residential units that he owns in an enfranchising building. This is referred to as exercising his right to a leaseback. If the landlord wishes to get a leaseback on one or more of his flats, he must state this in the counter-notice. This means that the leaseholders do not pay for these flats when they purchase the freehold. If the landlord does not wish to get a leaseback on his flats, the enfranchisers must buy these flats from the landlord at a fair market price as part of the enfranchisement process.

Whether or not the enfranchisers wish to buy any flats owned by the landlord, they must include in the enfranchisement notice a reasonable offer for these flats, as part of the total offer price. A failure to do so introduces a serious risk that the landlord will seek to have the enfranchisement notice declared invalid by filing a claim in the County court and alleging in the claim that the offer price is so low as to be unrealistic. The importance of presenting an offer price that can be substantiated with valuation evidence prepared by a qualified chartered surveyor is addressed in the section below on 'County court challenges by the landlord'.

Deemed withdrawals

One benefit that the enfranchisement legislation provides to leaseholders is the strict statutory timeframe. This enables a well-organised group of leaseholders to initiate and complete an enfranchisement within an identified period of time and to ensure the landlord does not create undue delays. But the statutory timeframe also creates risks that a poorly-organised leaseholder group will miss essential deadlines. If the leaseholders miss a statutory deadline, such as applying to the LVT no sooner than two months and no later than six months after a counter-notice has been received, this is seen as a 'deemed withdrawal'. A deemed withdrawal means that it is considered by law that the leaseholders have withdrawn their enfranchisement notice. If this happens, then the leaseholders are not allowed to serve a new enfranchisement notice for one year.

Other events that count as deemed withdrawals are:

- a move by the leaseholder group voluntarily to drop its enfranchisement initiative;

- failure to provide the landlord on request with the original deeds of participating flats for inspection within a ten-day written notice period, following the serving of an enfranchisement notice;

- failure to provide the landlord on request with access to inspect participating flats within a ten-day written notice period, following the serving of an enfranchisement notice; and

- failure to proceed to buy the freehold, once the LVT has announced the sale price.

County court challenges by the landlord

It is the LVT that decides at the end of the process on the price at which the landlord will sell the freehold. But the landlord has a right to challenge whether an offer price contained in an enfranchisement notice is realistic. If a landlord believes an offer price is so low as to be unrealistic or wishes to claim this, he can file a claim in the County court. This right is meant to protect the landlord against having to entertain silly offers, such as £1. If the landlord wishes to file such a claim in the County court, he must do so before an LVT hearing is held. If the landlord files this type of claim in the County court, the LVT will wait until the court case has been concluded before holding the LVT hearing. Leaseholders must take care, therefore, to include in their enfranchisement notice an offer price that is realistic.

If the landlord is successful in filing such a claim, that is, if the County court declares the offer price so low as to be unrealistic, then the court will declare the enfranchisement notice invalid. This means that the leaseholders must wait one year before beginning the enfranchisement process again.

The ability of landlords to delay or derail enfranchisements by filing these types of claims in the County court is a highly-contentious subject. Many leaseholders argue that this legal right, while meant to protect landlords against having to handle frivolous offer prices for their building, has instead been used to intimidate leaseholders by driving up their legal costs, and increasing the amount of time and effort required to push through an enfranchisement. Such increased costs, delays and distraction can easily demoralise enfranchisers and prompt one or more participants to drop out. By applying this type of pressure, a landlord can make a group of enfranchisers more amenable to reach a negotiated settlement without proceeding to the LVT. Many residents' associations feel that the LVT should be the one and only forum in which enfranchisement issues are decided. However, the law, as it exists, is meant to provide the LVT as the simpler, lower-cost quasi-judicial body responsible for deciding freehold costs, while also providing access for landlords and leaseholders in extreme circumstances to the legally-binding County court.

It should be noted that leaseholders also have the right to challenge the reasonableness of the landlord's counter-offer price, by filing their own claim in the County court. By doing this, enfranchisers ask the court to declare the landlord's counter-notice invalid on the grounds that it is so high as to be unrealistic. If the court finds in the enfranchisers' favour, they would be able to buy the building freehold at their initial offer price. However, in practice, very few leaseholders follow this route because of the additional legal costs and procedural complexity involved. In cases where leaseholders are unable to reach a negotiated agreement with the landlord after serving the enfranchisement notice and receiving the counter-notice, most prefer to take their enfranchisement straight to the LVT and to have the Tribunal decide on the price.

Negotiated acquisition

Leaseholders may wish to explore the possibility of buying the freehold of their building from the landlord through a negotiated acquisition, without ever serving an enfranchisement notice. However, they should be careful not to allow the landlord to use the possibility of a negotiated deal as a delaying tactic. If the landlord says he is willing to sell, the leaseholders should get a valuation done and then require that the landlord produce the necessary sales documentation within an identified timeframe, such as one month. If the landlord is unable to do so, leaseholders that wish to enfranchise should start the process.

Leaseholders that have already started an enfranchisement process by serving an enfranchisement notice have the right to reach a negotiated purchase agreement with the landlord at any time. But the sales documentation should be well in place before the leaseholders take any action to withdraw their enfranchisement notice.

A vast majority of enfranchisements are concluded with a negotiated agreement between the landlord and the residents' group before the process reaches the LVT. It is believed that some 200 enfranchisements end in negotiated acquisitions for every one enfranchisement that makes it all the way through to an LVT hearing. Many LVT applications are concluded with a negotiated acquisition just a few days before the scheduled LVT hearing.

Case study A in Appendix 2, 'Case studies' describes a residents' group that bought their building freehold by negotiated acquisition with the landlord after the enfranchisement notice and counter-notice had been served.

Tax relief for landlords in enfranchisements

Leaseholders should note that there is a Capital Gains Tax incentive for landlords to sell their building freehold or individual lease extensions through the statutory enfranchisement route rather than by negotiated agreement. The Inland Revenue announced on 17 September 1993 that landlords who were forced to sell a building freehold or a lease extension under the Leasehold Reform Act 1967 or the Leasehold Reform, Housing and Urban Development Act 1993 could claim tax rollover relief on the capital gains made from the sale. The Inland Revenue said in the announcement that this was similar to the rollover tax relief landlords were allowed to claim under Section 247 of the Taxation of Chargeable Gains Act 1992, where a landlord disposes of land to an authority in a compulsory transaction.

Therefore, when leaseholders are trying to get their landlord to agree to a negotiated sale of the freehold or an individual lease extension, they should keep in mind that the landlord has little, if any, Capital Gains Tax incentive to agree to such a sale unless he has first been served an enfranchisement notice by the relevant leaseholders.

Appealing against an LVT decision

Once the LVT has made its decision and has ordered a landlord to sell the freehold to the enfranchisers at a specific price, either party may appeal against the decision by taking the case to the Lands Tribunal. However, a party wishing to appeal to the Lands Tribunal must do so within 28 days of the LVT decision, must have so-called reasonable grounds for doing so and must gain written permission first from the LVT or the Lands Tribunal to make the appeal.

Freehold and leasehold

Leaseholders should remember that, once the freehold has been purchased through an enfranchisement process or any other process, the building will still have a freehold title and individual leasehold titles for each flat. A leaseholder that has participated in an enfranchisement will, after the purchase has been completed, continue to have a leasehold flat, and he will also be a shareholder of the new landlord company, i.e. the new freeholder. It is the freehold company that may grant lease extensions to participating and non-participating leasehold flats in the building. The freehold company normally grants 999-year leases to participating flats, that is the shareholders, at a nominal cost such as £1 plus legal fees after the enfranchisement process has been concluded.

The future changes in legislation

When the Commonhold and Leasehold Reform Act 2002 was passed, it contained several clauses that did not take immediate effect. These were parts of the law that needed secondary legislation in order to become enforceable. This secondary legislation has been put in place in a phased manner since 2002. At the time of writing, some final aspects of the 2002 Act had still not taken effect. There are two such delayed parts of the law that have particular importance for enfranchisers.

The first of these relates to the type of company that enfranchisers must set up. At present, most enfranchisers set up a limited company. This is a fairly straightforward process, whether it is done by enfranchisers themselves, a company formation firm or another agent. In the future, however, it is expected that enfranchisers will have to set up a new type of company, a so-called right-to-enfranchise or RTE company. This will have prescribed Memorandum and Articles of Association. The company must use the 'MemArts' set out by law and it cannot change them.

The second of the two expected legislative changes relates to the invitation to leaseholders in a building to participate in an enfranchisement. At present, there is no legal obligation to invite all leaseholders to participate. It is, nonetheless, best practice to do so. It is also best practice to communicate a clearly-defined deadline for the sign-up process. However, one legislative change that is expected later on is to give all leaseholders in a building the legal right to participate in an enfranchisement at any point, including up until the moment of conclusion of the freehold purchase.

Deciding whether to enfranchise or pursue other options

Buying the freehold of one's building presents the resident with certain opportunities and certain costs. There are two main compelling benefits for participants. Firstly, the leaseholders, in collectively becoming the new freeholder, gain full ownership and control over the building. This gives the participating residents greater ability to ensure proper management and maintenance of the building, cost accountability in carrying out such work, and building improvements that can enhance quality of life.

Secondly, the purchase of a building freehold enhances the value of participants' flats. This usually happens in three ways. Firstly, shareholder flats become more valuable because these leaseholders are now able to grant themselves 999-year leases. Secondly, buyers have been seen increasingly willing to pay a premium for flats in resident-owned buildings. Thirdly, leaseholders often carry out improvements after the freehold purchase, such as enhancing the porterage, replacing the carpet or giving the lobby a facelift, and these improvements again increase the value of the residential units.

The process of collective enfranchisement, however, is not a cost-free exercise. It is a commercial venture that is entered into by a group of residents. Like any financial investment, it carries a degree of risk. For all participants, there is a financial cost. For the organisers, there is also a hidden cost in terms of time and effort. It is important for the organisers and other participants to assess this from the start, since organisers are often expected to donate significant amounts of their time in organising and project managing an enfranchisement.

Leaseholders should pursue collective enfranchisement only after determining that this is the best option to pursue. Other options to be considered for a residential building include getting lease extensions and/or the right to manage. Although enfranchisement delivers to leaseholders full ownership of the building, which includes full management rights and the right to extend leases, it also demands that a higher price be paid in terms of money, time and effort.

The table below illustrates the comparative costs and benefits of collective enfranchisement (CE), as compared to lease extensions (LE) and securing the right to manage (RTM).

INPUT	CE	LE	RTM
Effort	✔✔✔✔	✔	✔✔
Organisation	✔✔✔	✔	✔✔
Cost	✔✔✔	✔✔✔	✔
OUTCOME			
Control	✔✔✔✔	✔	✔✔
Value capture	✔✔✔✔	✔✔✔	✔

While enfranchisement carries a higher price tag and requires greater organisational effort, it is also the only strategic choice that delivers the combined benefits of all three options at the end.

In this chapter we have described the rights of leaseholders in England and Wales to compel their landlord to sell to them the freehold of their building, and to do so at a fair price and within a statutory timeframe. Although some organisational challenges remain for leaseholders who wish to enfranchise, the 2002 Act has made it easier for flat owners to exercise this new legal right. In addition, the increasing numbers of leaseholder groups that are choosing to enfranchise have created a growing body of market knowledge on best practice and the most efficient ways in which to achieve success.

Absent landlords

Some leaseholders have the problem of not being able to locate their freeholder. If the whereabouts of the landlord are unknown, there is a procedure by which leaseholders can buy their building freehold. The process is similar to enfranchising the building, except that there is no landlord on whom an enfranchisement notice is served. There is also no landlord, of course, to dispute the leaseholders' offer price. The main steps of the process are:

1. Get a valuation of the freehold done.

2. Write to the County court to seek a so-called vesting order, which is a legal dispensation from having to serve an enfranchisement notice on the landlord. The court must be satisfied that the leaseholders qualify to enfranchise and that the landlord cannot reasonably be served an enfranchisement notice.

3. Apply to the LVT for a determination of the freehold price. This is called a Section 26 procedure, following the relevant piece of legislation.

4. Upon receiving the LVT decision, pay the LVT-stated freehold cost to the County court, usually to a district judge.

The LVT hearing at which the price of the freehold is determined in this type of case often lasts only a couple of hours, since there is no landlord to challenge the leaseholders' offer price.

Commonhold

When the 2002 Act was passed, it introduced a new type of commonhold ownership that sparked excitement amongst some flat owners. In a commonhold building, the owners of flats possess the freehold of their individual units in perpetuity and collectively they own all common parts of the building. With commonhold, there are no longer any leases for individual flats. In fact, the leasehold system is dropped entirely. Commonhold ownership of a building by residents is similar to the condo system in the United States.

Commonhold is brand new, since this aspect of the voluminous 2002 Act only took effect on 27 September 2004. Even so, there has been no visible move to embrace it. The reasons for this are clear. Firstly, in order for leaseholders of an existing block of flats to adopt commonhold ownership, they must first enfranchise the building and then they must unanimously approve the adoption of commonhold. Despite several clear attractions offered by commonhold ownership, as compared to the antiquated and inefficient leasehold system, it is highly unusual for residents in a building with more than two or three flats to achieve unanimity on this type of important issue.

Another reason this new type of joint building ownership has not yet taken off is that the law provides leaseholders with no ability to compel the landlord to convert a building into commonhold. Residents must follow the two-step process of first enfranchising and then converting the building themselves into commonhold.

Industry experts say that the government had expected newly-constructed apartment buildings to be commonhold, but this trend has not emerged. Property developers consider that there is little, if any, financial incentive for them to construct commonhold buildings, since buyers of flats are not presently demanding this. In addition, the old leasehold system enables the developer to sell the leasehold units, while maintaining ownership and control of the building as the freeholder.

If commonhold does become more achievable later on, it will simplify life for flat owners. According to statutory regulations, the commonhold flat owner, or 'unit-holder', is a member of a so-called Commonhold Association in the building. The Commonhold Association is a limited company with prescribed Memorandum and Articles of Association. The Association is governed by provisions of the 2002 Act, the Commonhold Regulations 2004 and a document called the Commonhold Community Statement, the form and contents of which are also prescribed.

The Commonhold Community Statement defines the duties and responsibilities of the Commonhold Association in the building and of each unit-holder. There is just the one document for the building and, happily for flat owners, no more leases. Owners of commonhold flats escape the wasting-asset problem of leasehold, since they own the freehold of their units forever. By eliminating the concept of the third-party landlord, residents are also able to have the building maintained and run as they wish.

CHAPTER 4

Calculating the freehold price

One of the questions most frequently asked by leaseholders that are considering buying their freehold, getting lease extensions or gaining the right to manage is 'How much will it cost?' This chapter provides a practical overview of the principles involved in valuing a freehold for a collective enfranchisement. These same principles apply when a leaseholder exercises his legal right to compel the landlord to sell a 90-year lease extension, at a fair price and within a statutory timeframe. This is because buying a 90-year lease extension means, in essence, that the leaseholder is enfranchising just the one flat. More information on this is provided in chapter 5, 'Lease extensions'.

In this chapter we aim to provide leaseholders and others interested in enfranchisement with an understanding of the valuation formula and its elements, and valuation issues that arise in enfranchisement cases. While this book is meant to convey must-have information to the layperson, it does not eliminate the need for a qualified surveyor in carrying out a formal valuation of a freehold. Leaseholders are strongly urged to instruct an experienced surveyor when having a valuation done for the purpose of enfranchising one's building.

Valuation principles

Enfranchisement legislation prescribes a formula for calculating the value of a freehold. While the average layperson may find the formula overly-complex, the principle behind it is simple. It is aimed at calculating the value in the building that the landlord will lose as a result of being forced to sell the freehold, and then calculating the amount that leaseholders must pay to the landlord, by way of fair compensation. The formula is aimed at ensuring that leaseholders pay a fair price and that landlords receive a fair price. It is meant to protect the interests of both sides in this compulsory sale, which is by its nature an adversarial commercial transaction.

Leaseholder versus freeholder interest

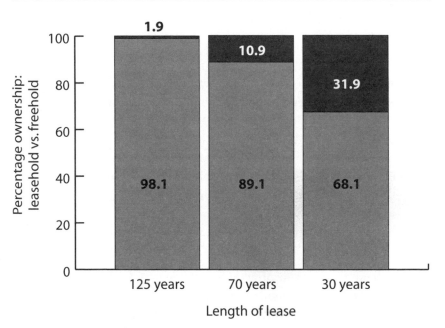

Source of data: Savills Research

Leaseholders might consider that the market value of their flat at any point in time represents the entire value of the unit. This is not the case. Each leasehold flat has two ownership elements, that of the leaseholder and that of the freeholder. For this reason we say that a flat has a leasehold interest and a freehold interest. Because of the wasting-asset principle, a flat that is worth £500,000 to the leaseholder today will be worth zero pounds to the same leaseholder once the lease expires, because full ownership and full value will revert to the landlord. The diagram above illustrates the manner in which the leasehold interest in a flat is considered to decrease as a proportion of the total value and the landlord interest increases as the lease term diminishes. While valuers' estimates vary, according to these sample numbers from Savills Research, the leasehold interest represents 98.1 per cent of the freehold interest when there are 125 years left on the lease, but this decreases to 89.1 per cent and 68.1 per cent when there are only 70 and 30 years left respectively.

A main task for the surveyor in an enfranchisement is to calculate the total value of the combined leasehold and freehold interests. This equals the value of the flat once the freehold has been bought, since the leaseholder will then own both leasehold and freehold interests. The leasehold interest is often called the 'tenant's interest' and the freehold interest is often called the 'landlord's interest'. The surveyor must also calculate the value of the future expected event in which, when the term of the lease expires, full ownership of the flat will revert to the landlord. This expected event in the future has a value today, which is called the 'reversion'. For this reason, the landlord is sometimes referred to as the 'reversioner'.

The formula for valuing a freehold

There are three main elements comprising the freehold valuation:

1. The landlord's interest: the income stream from future ground rent.

2. The landlord's interest: the value of the reversion.

3. The so-called 'marriage value' of participating flats, where marriage value is payable.

In calculating the landlord's interest, one is calculating what the landlord stands to lose in having to sell the freehold. The landlord's interest is calculated in two steps for the purpose of an enfranchisement. Firstly, by being forced to sell the freehold, the landlord will no longer receive the income stream, year after year, in the form of ground rent paid by all leaseholders in the building. The landlord will also lose the reversion value, because he will no longer be able to expect that the leasehold flats will revert to his ownership when the leases expire.

We have seen that, as the expiry date of a lease grows nearer, the landlord's reversion value increases. This explains why a prospective buyer of a flat with a lease that has less than 50 years left can have difficulty securing a mortgage, because the mortgage lender sees that the reversion is not far away.

In an enfranchisement, the landlord is entitled to be paid by the nominee purchaser 100 per cent of the capitalised rate of the landlord's interest. This is explained below.

Marriage value

Marriage value is a term frequently used when discussing freehold valuation. It refers to the value that is created in a flat as a result of combining, or marrying, the freehold and leasehold elements of the property, that is, when leaseholders buy the freehold and become the freeholder. For example, a leasehold flat might have a market value of £100,000 before the freehold is bought by the leaseholders and it might have a market value of £110,000 after the freehold has been bought. Although the formula for calculating marriage value is more complex than this, the £10,000 in newly-created value is, roughly speaking, the marriage value. The reason that marriage value is created in an enfranchisement is because the leaseholder, as a partial owner of the new freehold company, can get a 999-year lease extension for a nominal fee after the freehold purchase has been completed. This lease extension automatically increases the value of the flat.

In an enfranchisement, the landlord is entitled to be paid by the nominee purchaser 50 per cent of the marriage value of applicable flats.

In an enfranchisement it is only the marriage value of participating flats that is counted. Marriage value of non-participating flats does not figure in the calculation of the value of the freehold. Marriage value is also only applicable on participating flats that have less than 80 years on their leases. There is no marriage value payable on any participating flats where the lease has 80 years or more to run.

Although we defined marriage value above in an abbreviated manner, one must quantify four components in order to carry out a correct calculation of the marriage value. These components are:

Present value

(a) The tenant's interest (this is the market value of the flat today)

(b) The landlord's interest (this is the capitalised amount of the ground rent and reversion)

Future value

(c) The tenant's interest (this is the estimated value of the flat with an extended lease)

(d) The landlord's interest (this is zero once the freehold has been bought)

The tenant's interest is the estimated market value of the flat today. To calculate the landlord's interest, one must calculate the present value (the value today) of the income stream from ground rent that the landlord will lose and the present value of the future reversion to his ownership of the flats when the leases expire. To make these calculations, one uses a yield (also referred to as the discount rate or capitalisation rate) over the period of time left on the leases, and a present value table, such as the one provided in Appendix 6, 'Present value table'. Regarding the ground rent, one is calculating the amount of money one would need to have today to compensate for the lost income stream of ground rent over the years. Regarding the reversion, one is calculating the amount of money one would need to have today to compensate for the loss of the reversion at the end of the leases. Since the 1990s many landlords with prime property in central London have sought to apply a lower discount rate, say six per cent or lower, while enfranchisers often argue for a higher discount rate of nine or ten per cent. A lower discount rate will result in a higher freehold valuation figure, while a higher discount rate will result in a lower valuation figure.

Once the four components above have been quantified, the marriage value is calculated by adding the tenant's interest and the landlord's interest after the freehold acquisition, then subtracting from that the value of the tenant's interest and the landlord's interest today. In other words, the formula for marriage value is:

$$MV = (c+d) - (a+b)$$

The nominee purchaser must pay the landlord one-half of this marriage value and all of the present value of the landlord's interest, that is:

$$\text{Freehold value} = 1/2MV + (b)$$

Development value and hope value

The landlord may claim that there is other value he is losing, beyond the capitalised ground rent and reversion, and marriage value. These can include so-called 'development value' and 'hope value'. Development value is the value to the landlord today of a future development of the property. For instance, a landlord may claim that he had planned to build two additional storeys onto a block of flats that is being enfranchised. He might say that he had planned to sell the resulting eight new flats and that he should now be compensated because he will no longer be able to pursue this development. Or the landlord might say that he had planned to build and sell garages behind the building and he might demand that the enfranchisers compensate him for the money that he will now lose. Some landlords have been reported to seek planning permission for constructing additional storeys on residential blocks in order to increase the value of the freehold when residents enfranchise.

A landlord's claim for compensation for development value can result in his freehold valuation differing dramatically from that of the nominee purchaser. This is discussed in more detail in the section below on 'Sample valuations from LVT cases'.

Hope value is a valuation element that refers to the so-called hope by the new landlord, the enfranchisers, that non-participating leaseholders will seek to get their leases extended after the freehold has been bought. While the idea normally is for participants in an enfranchisement to get 999-year lease extensions from their new freehold company for a nominal cost, such as £1 plus legal fees, a usual practice in large blocks of flats is for non-participants to be charged a commercial rate for a 90-year lease extension after the freehold purchase has been completed. Therefore, if, for instance, only 20 out of a total 30 leaseholders in a building participate in an enfranchisement, the landlord might seek to be compensated by the nominee purchaser for what he claims is the hope value for the nominee purchaser to sell 90-year lease extensions to each of the ten non-participants at a commercial price, after the freehold has been bought.

Leaseholders who are seeking to address the issue of hope value from the beginning and to manage an enfranchisement in the most fair and democratic manner normally send a written invitation to all leaseholders in the building, offering the opportunity to join in the enfranchisement. If only 20 of a total 30 leaseholders subsequently decide to join in the freehold purchase initiative, the nominee purchaser may later seek to present such documentation, including the original invitation sent to all leaseholders, as evidence at a Leasehold Valuation Tribunal (LVT) hearing that indicates the ten non-participants cannot reasonably be expected to seek to buy lease extensions any time soon.

Debating points in valuations

Although the surveyor working for a landlord will sometimes come up with a valuation that is close to that produced by the leaseholders' surveyor, the two figures often differ. As we will see below, landlords often demand a price for the freehold that is several times higher than the price offered by enfranchising leaseholders. Main elements that produce the largest discrepancies between leaseholders' and landlords' valuations are:

* the estimated market value of the flats;

* the yield used;

* the development value; and

* the hope value.

Regarding the estimated market value of the flats, it is not unusual for the landlord to claim that the flats in the building have a higher market value than that claimed by the leaseholders. Since one element used in calculating marriage value is the estimated market value of participating flats, it is important for enfranchising leaseholders to keep as complete a record as possible of sales values in the building and related information, such as sales figures of comparable flats in other buildings. Of course, market values in buildings will vary according to location, the state of repair, the length of leases and other elements.

While landlords often push for lower yields, which implies that the freehold purchase is a lower-risk investment, many leaseholders argue for higher yields because they view the acquisition of the building as a higher-risk venture. It is easy to see why residents would make this argument if, for instance, their building is 100 years old, in extreme need of major repairs and plagued by a history of disputes in which residents have refused to pay service charges to the landlord. LVT decisions in recent years have been based on yields mostly ranging from six to 11 per cent.

When development and/or hope value feature in an enfranchisement, it is normally the landlord who is arguing that one or both of these values exist, while the leaseholders argue that they do not. It is important for each side to document carefully why it is making the argument that it is making. Enfranchising leaseholders in a 100-year-old purpose-built mansion block might argue that there is no development value on the roof, if the roof is in serious need of repair and the building is located in a conservation area that would make it unlikely to obtain planning permission. Leaseholders in such cases can strengthen their argument by obtaining documentation from local authorities showing that no such proposed construction on the roof is likely to receive planning approval.

Relativity tables versus market comparables

Landlords sometimes produce higher valuations for a freehold than leaseholders because their surveyors have made more extensive use of documents called relativity tables. A relativity table lists estimated values of leasehold properties as a proportion of the freehold interest, as we saw above in the section on 'Leaseholder versus freeholder interest'. The relativity table issued by Savills Research, which is provided in Appendix 5, 'Relativity table', includes the following estimated values:

Number of years left on lease	Percentage of extended lease value
125	98.1
90	95.3
80	92.4
70	89.1
60	85.2
50	80.7
40	75.2

30	68.1
20	58.0
10	40.9

Source of data: Savills Research

One sees many instances in which surveyors working for landlords use relativity tables to argue that flats have greater marriage value than that claimed by the leaseholders' surveyor. Surveyors working for leaseholders are often more likely to rely on real market data, that is, the sale prices of comparable flats located nearby. In enfranchisement cases, these data are called 'market comparables'.

If there are significant discrepancies in valuations, each side should do its best to present a reasonable number of relevant market comparables, since these can provide a strong indication of the market value of the flats in the enfranchising building.

Informal freehold valuation

Enfranchisement organisers often face an awkward situation when trying to estimate, at the early stage, the eventual cost of the freehold. They will want to include some cost estimate in the document that they send to all leaseholders, inviting them to participate in the enfranchisement. However, organisers will not normally want to spend money on getting a formal valuation done unless a minimum of 50 per cent of all the flats have signed up for the enfranchisement and have paid a deposit to secure their place in the enfranchisement project. Therefore, the organisers and other leaseholders are faced with a chicken-and-egg dilemma. Leaseholders may be reluctant to sign up until they have seen a proper cost estimate, but no proper cost estimate is likely to be prepared until enough residents have put deposit money into the pot to hire a valuer.

There are three easy methods for making quick informal freehold valuations, for the purpose of getting a rough idea about the cost of the freehold. The first is to invite a number of surveyors to the building for an introductory meeting. This meeting enables leaseholders to decide whether to hire the surveyor later on to do a formal valuation. It also provides an opportunity to seek from the surveyor an informal ballpark figure regarding the cost of the freehold. Many surveyors are willing to give this type of informal estimate, as long as it is made clear that it does not represent a formal valuation.

The second quick method is for enfranchisers to ask several estate agents in the area for an estimate of the added value to one or more flats in the building if leases are extended by 90 years. This estimated added value equates roughly to the marriage value of a flat. Enfranchisers can then take this figure, apply it to each expected participant flat and divide the result by two. This figure, again, represents a rough estimate of the marriage value, which is usually the largest component of the freehold cost in enfranchisements where there is marriage value.

Finally, leaseholders can work out a quick informal valuation by plugging the relevant numbers from their building into the formulae provided in the sections above on 'The formula for valuing a freehold' and 'Marriage value'. When doing the calculation, leaseholders can use a six per cent yield as a worst-case cost scenario and a ten per cent yield as a best-case scenario.

It is important to remember that these informal valuation methods do not eliminate the need at some stage for a proper formal valuation to be done by a qualified chartered surveyor with solid enfranchisement experience, before leaseholders proceed with an enfranchisement initiative.

Sample valuations from LVT cases

While the formula for calculating the value of a freehold is complex and prescribed by law, leaseholders need to keep in mind the fact that such valuations can be more of an art than a science. Leaseholders often offer a lower freehold price in their enfranchisement notice and landlords frequently demand a higher price in their counter-notice, but both sides usually end in a negotiated deal after haggling over various cost elements.

Many building freeholds over the past decade have sold for less than £10,000. The cheapest freehold, as determined by an LVT decision between 1994 and 2004, was a four-flat building in the Southgate area of North London. On 23 September 2004, the LVT ordered the landlord, Verkan Company Limited, to sell the freehold of 143, 145, 147 and 149 The

Vale to the building's enfranchising leaseholders for a mere £50. The leases in this building had about 140 years left, as the residents had bought lease extensions two years earlier. At the other end of the cost spectrum, the biggest freehold price tag was announced by the LVT on 14 August 2002 for an 82-flat block near London's Hyde Park. The LVT ordered the landlord, the Church Commissioners for England, to sell the freehold of 25–31 Hyde Park Gardens and 22–35 Stanhope Terrace to the building's 54 participating residents for £6,586,857. The leases in this building had just over 40 years to run.

A review of decisions made by the LVT on enfranchisement cases since 1994 reveals an often staggering difference between freehold prices offered by residents and those demanded by landlords. The table below, which contains data from 12 sample cases, shows that landlords often demand prices that are many times greater than the leaseholders' offer price.

Price offered by tenants for freehold (£)	Price demanded by landlord for freehold (£)	Price of freehold determined by LVT (£)	Landlord price demanded, as percentage of tenant offer price	LVT price, as percentage of tenant offer price	Landlord price demanded, as percentage of LVT determined price
7,152	14,531	12,150	203	170	120
5,150	11,000	10,200	214	198	108
1,500	100,000	1,580	6,667	105	6,329
1,655	5,000	1,655	302	100	302
23,879	212,000	37,000	888	155	573
16,600	46,800	22,600	282	136	207
6,970	12,600	7,045	181	101	179
2,850	10,950	2,850	384	100	384
2,000	19,848	6,530	992	327	304
35,000	73,000	50,400	209	144	145
53,080	933,000	131,172	1,758	247	711
2,000	540,000	4,135	27,000	207	13,059

Source of data: Residential Property Tribunal Service

Some of the biggest discrepancies between leaseholders' and landlords' valuations relate to development value. In many of these instances, the landlords have claimed that they were losing out on the ability to develop the property, for instance, by building additional storeys on top. In the case of 44 Fellows Road, a four-storey converted house in London's Camden area, the enfranchisers offered £24,200 for the freehold. But the landlord demanded nearly ten times this amount at £211,300. The LVT, however, ordered the landlord on 27 April 2000 to sell the freehold for £76,700 and rejected the landlord's demand for development value for additional flats it supposedly planned to build on the roof.

Making a realistic offer

The law does not require that leaseholders make an offer price for a freehold that represents their final offer or even that they offer the price that they expect to pay. It is understood that leaseholders will often present a lower offer price and landlords will demand a higher counter-offer price. But as we have seen in chapter 3, 'Buying the freehold', leaseholders must take care to offer a price that is realistic, and that can be substantiated by valuation evidence. This is in order to avoid encouraging the landlord to file a claim in the County court alleging that the offer price is so low as to be unrealistic. As discussed above, if the landlord is successful in convincing the County court that the offer price is unrealistic, then the court will declare the original enfranchisement notice invalid and the leaseholders will have to wait another year before beginning the enfranchisement process again.

CHAPTER 5

Lease extensions

One of the biggest problems affecting the leaseholder is the fact that the net value of his leasehold property diminishes every year, as the term of the lease runs down. While growing numbers of leaseholders are addressing this issue by joining forces with neighbours to buy the building freehold through collective enfranchisement, another important option is to purchase a lease extension. While the process can prove unwieldy, leaseholders have a legal right to compel their landlord to sell them a 90-year lease extension. Changes in legislation in recent years have expanded this right and made the process more straightforward. This chapter describes the process of buying a lease extension and explains the circumstances in which a lease extension can represent a more logical option for leaseholders than buying the freehold.

Extending one's lease

Most leaseholders of flats in England and Wales are allowed by law to compel their landlord to sell them a 90-year lease extension, which gets added on to the number of years remaining on the existing lease, and to do so for a fair price within a statutory timeframe. The laws that provide this right for flat owners are the Leasehold Reform, Housing and Urban Development Act 1993, the Housing Act 1996 and the Commonhold and Leasehold Reform Act 2002.

Securing a lease extension increases the value of a leasehold property, since it combines the existing market value of the flat, that is, the 'leaseholder's interest', described in chapter 4, 'Calculating the freehold price', with the freeholder's interest. Indeed, buying a 90-year lease extension is considered by law the enfranchisement of a single flat, since the leaseholder is, in essence, buying the freehold element of the flat. Although the purchase of a lease extension does not deliver the multiple benefits of collective enfranchisement, since the leaseholder does not gain ownership and control over the building, it can be a useful tool for protecting and enhancing the value of the flat.

While the law guarantees leaseholders the right to secure a 90-year lease extension, they are, of course, also free to reach a negotiated agreement with the landlord regarding the purchase of a lease extension for 90 years, or for a shorter or longer period of time.

Qualifying for a lease extension

In order to compel a landlord to sell a 90-year lease extension, the leaseholder and the leaseholder's building must qualify. Not all buildings and residents qualify for the legal right to a lease extension. It is important to confirm, before beginning the formal process, that the building and leaseholder both qualify.

The building qualification for a lease extension

A building will be eligible for individual lease extensions if:

1. it is a residential structure, not a commercial building;

2. it is not within the precinct boundary of a cathedral; and

3. it is not owned by a charitable housing trust, the National Trust or the Crown.

The resident qualification for a lease extension

A resident will qualify for a 90-year lease extension if:

1. he has a 'long lease', that is, the lease term was for more than 21 years at the time it was granted;

2. he has owned the lease for at least two years at the time of serving notice on the landlord for a lease extension; and

3. he is not a business or commercial tenant.

If a leaseholder is in doubt about qualification, he should contact the Leasehold Advisory Service. Contact details are provided in Appendix 1, 'Useful contacts'.

The main phases of the lease extension process

There are five phases in the formal process of demanding, through the statutory route, that a landlord sell a 90-year lease extension. These are similar to the collective enfranchisement process described in chapter 3, 'Buying the freehold', although buying a lease extension is simpler since only one flat is involved. While the official lease extension process comprises five phases, it should be noted that most residents' requests for a lease extension are concluded in a negotiated settlement with the landlord and do not go all the way to the Leasehold Valuation Tribunal (LVT). Because there are strict deadlines established by law for the landlord and for the leaseholder when a lease extension is being sought, it is essential to complete all the required preparations before starting the formal process. The five phases are described below.

The preparatory stage

Before beginning the formal process of requesting a lease extension, the leaseholder must identify the name and address of the freeholder. If the leaseholder is in doubt, a quick online search at HM Land Registry, at www.landregisteronline.gov.uk, will normally produce the information. Failing this, leaseholders have the legal right to be provided this information by the landlord and they can serve a formal notice on the landlord requiring that they be provided with this information. This right is contained in Section 41 of the Leasehold Reform, Housing and Urban

Development Act 1993, and the form that must be sent to the landlord is usually called a Section 41 Notice. A copy of this notice is contained in the 'Forms and other useful documents' section. The Section 41 Notice is also used in order to find out from the landlord whether he has been served an enfranchisement notice, also called a Section 13 Notice, by the leaseholders. A template for the Section 41 Notice is provided in Appendix 7, 'Information request prior to a lease extension'. If the landlord has been served an enfranchisement notice by the leaseholders, he is not allowed to sell or otherwise grant lease extensions for the duration of the enfranchisement process.

In preparing to request a lease extension, the resident needs to have a valuation done of the flat and the sought lease extension. Although it is not required by law to hire a chartered surveyor to do this work, it is strongly recommended to instruct a surveyor with solid expertise and experience in collective enfranchisement and lease extensions. The surveyor should inspect the property and then prepare a formal confidential valuation report, in which the leaseholder is advised of the estimated value of a 90-year lease extension and which offer price to include in the notice.

Finally, the resident should also instruct a solicitor, who needs to prepare and serve on the landlord the notice that requests the 90-year lease extension. While it is not required by law to hire a solicitor for this work, leaseholders are strongly advised to do so and to hire a solicitor with a known track record in enfranchisement and lease extensions.

Phase 1: The tenant's notice

The formal process of requesting a lease extension begins when the initial notice is served by the leaseholder on the landlord. While most leaseholders do not consider themselves 'tenants', we refer here to the 'tenant's notice' since this is the legal term used, based on the fact that leasehold is a form of tenancy. The tenant's notice is also referred to as a Section 42 Notice, which refers to the relevant section of the 1993 Act. The tenant's notice must contain the leaseholder's offer price for the lease extension and the deadline by which the landlord must reply. By law, the landlord must reply within two months of the date of the tenant's notice. The notice must also identify the property and leaseholder in question, provide details of the lease, such as the date it started and the amount of ground rent payable, the terms to be provided in the new replacement lease, and the name and address of any appointed representative of the leaseholder. A sample tenant's notice is provided in Appendix 8, 'Lease extension notice'. The notice is normally served on the landlord by the leaseholder's solicitor.

Once the landlord has received the tenant's notice, he has the right to inspect the original lease. The landlord must send any such request within 21 days of the tenant's notice. The leaseholder must respond to any such request within 21 days. The landlord also has the right to inspect the flat, for the purpose of carrying out a valuation.

If the landlord misses the deadline stated in the tenant's notice, the leaseholder has the right to buy the lease extension at the offer price contained in the tenant's notice. To buy the lease extension in this manner, the leaseholder must apply to the County court within a maximum of six months. In applying to the County court, the leaseholder must ask for a so-called 'vesting order', by which the court declares that the landlord must sell the lease extension to the leaseholder at the offer price. It is unusual for large corporate landlords to miss the deadline for sending the counter-notice.

Phase 2: The landlord's counter-notice

Phase 2 starts with the counter-notice being served by the landlord on the leaseholder or the leaseholder's appointed representative. In the counter-notice, the landlord must:

1. acknowledge that the leaseholder has the right to a 90-year lease extension and agree with the offer price; or

2. acknowledge that the leaseholder has the right to a 90-year lease extension, but state a counter-offer price; or

3. challenge the right of the leaseholder to a 90-year lease extension.

Many freeholders select option 2, by acknowledging the right of the leaseholder to buy a lease extension, but demanding a higher price. In this case, the landlord must provide the counter-offer price in his counter-notice.

At any time after receiving the tenant's notice, the landlord is allowed to demand a deposit from the leaseholder. This can be ten per cent of the leaseholder's offer price or £250, whichever figure is higher.

Phase 3: The application to the LVT

Phase 3 of the lease extension process begins when the leaseholder or the landlord files an application with the LVT. Both parties have the right to do so, but it is normally the leaseholder that applies to the LVT. In making this application, the leaseholder is asking the LVT to decide on the price at which the landlord must sell the lease extension. If an application is to be made to the LVT, this must be done no sooner than two months and no later than six months after the date of the counter-notice. Leaseholders that do apply to the LVT usually do so through their solicitor.

The reason that the law bans an application being made to the LVT sooner than two months after the counter-notice is to provide sufficient time for both parties to hold negotiations and reach a negotiated agreement on the price. A large majority of lease extensions cases are concluded in this way, after the tenant's notice has been served and before an LVT hearing is held.

Phase 4: The LVT hearing and decision

Phase 4 begins when a hearing is held at the LVT. It usually takes three to four months from the time an application is sent to the LVT for a hearing to take place. LVT hearings for lease extensions usually take a maximum of one day. The LVT panel normally comprises three members, a lawyer, a surveyor and a layperson, although a panel can also comprise just two people. It is not required by law for the leaseholder to be represented at the LVT hearing by professional advisors, although many leaseholders choose to have a solicitor and/or surveyor speak on their behalf at the hearing. In some cases, a leaseholder might also instruct a barrister to be present at the hearing.

After the hearing, the LVT reaches its decision and sends its written determination to both parties. This document will contain the price at which the landlord must sell the lease extension to the leaseholder. The LVT determination becomes final after 28 days. If the leaseholder finds the price too high, he is not obliged to buy the lease extension. The leaseholder may decide to walk away from the deal and to drop the request for a lease extension.

Phase 5: The completion of the purchase of a lease extension

Once the LVT has sent its written determination, the landlord must provide a draft new lease to the leaseholder within 21 days. Within two months of the LVT decision, both parties must have entered into a new lease agreement. Although the new lease is basically the same as the old lease with 90 years added on to the remaining term, it is likely to contain a few minor revisions. These are described below.

If the landlord fails to provide the new draft lease or the new final lease within the above timeframes, the leaseholder can apply within the following two months to the County court, in order to ask the court to order the landlord to meet his obligations to provide the new lease.

The timeframe of lease extensions

Although buying a lease extension is a simpler process than collectively enfranchising one's building, since only one flat is involved, the statutory timeframe is similar to that of enfranchisement. This is because the law requires that each party has sufficient time to carry out the necessary work in applying for or handling a request for a lease extension. The table below shows a best-case schedule for buying a lease extension, if the leaseholder moves as rapidly as possible from one phase to the next.

Event	Month in which the event occurs
The tenant's notice is served on the landlord by the leaseholder	Month 1
The counter-notice is served on the leaseholder by the landlord	Month 3

The leaseholder applies to the LVT	Month 5
The LVT hearing is held	Month 8
The LVT decision is issued	Month 9

As we have seen, however, many lease extension requests are concluded more quickly than the eight-month timeframe presented above because negotiated settlements are often agreed in the weeks following the serving of a tenant's notice or landlord's counter-notice.

The costs involved in buying a lease extension

The costs for a leaseholder in buying a lease extension for his flat through the statutory route are:

* the lease extension itself;

* the leaseholder's solicitor and surveyor fees; and

* the landlord's solicitor and surveyor fees.

The leaseholder must pay the landlord's so-called 'reasonable costs' in handling the tenant's notice, and in preparing and serving the counter-notice. The landlord's costs are for his own solicitor and the surveyor that carries out the landlord's valuation of the lease extension. If a leaseholder feels that the landlord has charged unreasonable costs, then he can challenge these costs by making a separate application to the LVT. Hourly fees charged by solicitors in London that specialise in enfranchisement range from approximately £150 to over £400 per hour.

When a leaseholder applies to the LVT to get a lease extension, there is no application fee.

It is important to note that if a lease extension case goes all the way to an LVT hearing, each side pays its own way for this stage of the process. Any work done by the leaseholder's solicitor and/or surveyor in preparing for or attending an LVT hearing is paid for by the leaseholder, while the landlord pays his own LVT costs. It is because landlords must pay their own LVT costs that such a large majority of lease extension cases are concluded through negotiated settlement before an LVT hearing takes place.

A small minority of lease extension cases end up in the County court. This is discussed below, including an explanation of the payment of court costs.

As noted above, once the landlord has served a counter-notice in a lease extension case, he can demand a deposit from the leaseholder. This is calculated as a percentage of the offer price that is contained in the tenant's notice. A deposit of ten per cent or £250 may be demanded, whichever is the higher figure. It is important for leaseholders to avoid the temptation to present an absurdly-low offer price in the tenant's notice, in the hope of minimising the amount of deposit, since this can result in the lease extension case ending up in the County court and the tenant's notice being declared invalid by the court. This possible sequence of events is explained later in the chapter.

When considering whether to buy a lease extension or join an enfranchisement, the resident should keep in mind that the cost of a lease extension is usually comparable to the individual participant's cost in buying his share of the freehold in a collective enfranchisement.

Extending leases before collective enfranchisement

Some residents make the mistake of believing that buying lease extensions eliminates or places at risk the possibility, later on, for residents to buy the freehold of the building through the process of collective enfranchisement. Lease extensions and enfranchisement are options in a residential building that are not mutually exclusive. One or more residents may decide to buy lease extensions and then a minimum of 50 per cent of all flats in the building may subsequently decide to enfranchise. Those residents holding the newly-extended leases may decide to participate or not to participate in the enfranchisement.

When a leaseholder needs urgently to protect the value of a flat with a very low number of years left on the lease, buying a 90-year lease extension represents a simpler, easier and lower-risk option than enfranchisement, since the leaseholder is acting as an individual and is not dependent on the success of a group of fellow residents. If and when the other residents later proceed with the enfranchisement of the building, then participants holding the leases that have been extended by 90 years simply pay a lower price for their share of the freehold. This is because they have already, in essence, enfranchised their individual flats by buying the lease extensions. It is also for this reason that the freehold will cost less in a building where one or more residents have already bought lease extensions, since the landlord has already been obliged to sell his 'freeholder interest' in these individual flats to the relevant leaseholders. There is no marriage value to be paid for the newly-extended leases, of course, since they have more than 80 years left to run.

The success factors in lease extensions

This section identifies important issues that can arise when a leaseholder sets out to buy a lease extension through the statutory route. It also provides a guide for ensuring that the process moves forward in the smoothest, lowest-risk and most cost-effective manner.

Deemed withdrawals

The legislation that provides the right for a leaseholder to buy a 90-year lease extension and to do so at a fair price within a statutory timeframe provides the benefit of ensuring that landlords do not create unreasonable delays. However, as is the case with collective enfranchisement, leaseholders are also bound by strict legal deadlines. It is essential for leaseholders not to miss any of these deadlines, since this would equate to the leaseholder having withdrawn his tenant's notice. As we have seen with enfranchisements, such an event is called a 'deemed withdrawal'. If, for example, a leaseholder fails to apply to the LVT during the period from two to six months after the counter-notice, this is a deemed withdrawal. If there is a deemed withdrawal, the leaseholder is not allowed to begin the lease extension process again for 12 months.

Other events that count as deemed withdrawals are:

- a move by the leaseholder voluntarily to drop or withdraw his tenant's notice;

- a failure to provide the landlord with required information within 21 days after the tenant's notice has been served; and

- a failure to proceed to buy the lease extension, once the LVT has announced the sale price.

Appealing against an LVT decision

Once an LVT hearing has been held and the LVT has sent its written determination to both parties, either party can appeal against the decision. Appeals are heard in the Lands Tribunal. However, any appeal must be requested within 28 days of the LVT decision and can only be made after written permission has been obtained by the LVT or by the Lands Tribunal.

County court challenges by the landlord

Although it is not required by law for a leaseholder to instruct a chartered surveyor and a solicitor when seeking a lease extension, it is a practice that is strongly advised. Leaseholders should be careful to hire a surveyor and solicitor who have extensive experience and proven expertise in the related areas of collective enfranchisement and lease extensions. One reason for this is to minimise the chance of serving a tenant's notice on the landlord that could be declared invalid by a County court. For instance, the landlord has a right, if he believes the offer price contained in the tenant's notice to be so low as to be unrealistic, to file a claim in the County court in which he asks the court to declare the notice invalid. If the court declares a tenant's notice invalid, then the lease extension process stops and the leaseholder is not allowed to start the process again for 12 months. While this only happens in a small minority of lease extension cases, the possibility of this type of County court claim creates a strong disincentive for leaseholders to make lease extension offers that cannot be substantiated with valuation evidence.

If the landlord files this type of claim against the leaseholder in the County court, both sides pay their legal costs until the end of the process. At the end, the court may order the losing side to pay all or some of the legal and surveyor costs that were incurred in the court case by the winning side.

By law, the leaseholder is also protected against the landlord demanding an unrealistically high counter-offer price in the counter-notice. If a leaseholder files this type of claim in the County court and wins, he gets to buy the lease extension at the asking price. However, very few leaseholders file this type of claim in the County court because of the legal and surveyor fees, the time and effort involved, and the additional possible court costs if the leaseholder's claim fails. The vast majority, including those who feel that the landlord has demanded an absurdly high price, prefer to proceed to the LVT, in the expectation that the LVT will decide on a fair price.

Group discounts for several lease extensions

In buildings where more than one leaseholder wishes to buy a 90-year lease extension, these residents can join together informally and seek a group discount from a solicitor and surveyor for the work involved.

Seeking a lease extension during an enfranchisement process

If residents have begun the formal process of collectively enfranchising their building by serving an enfranchisement notice on the landlord, then the landlord is not allowed to sell any lease extensions until the enfranchisement process has been concluded. If a landlord receives a tenant's notice requesting a 90-year lease extension, the landlord must write to the relevant leaseholder and explain that no lease extensions can be sold because an enfranchisement process has started. The landlord must also notify the enfranchisers in writing about the request for the lease extension.

Selling a flat before the completion of the lease extension process

If a leaseholder has begun a lease extension process by serving a tenant's notice on the landlord and then decides to sell his flat before the process has been completed, the leaseholder can transfer or 'assign' to a buyer the right to the lease extension. This is an important right for sellers, since anyone buying a leasehold flat does not have the right to demand a 90-year lease extension until they have owned the flat for a minimum of two years.

Changes in the new lease

When the new extended lease is being prepared, the landlord must make a few changes to the wording that was contained in the old lease. These changes include:

- an insertion stating that the new lease is provided at a so-called 'peppercorn rent', that is, no ground rent;

- an insertion that refers to any important modifications made to the flat or building since the lease was created, such as reference to gas, lighting or other services that no longer exist;

- the deletion of any reference to the renewal or early termination of the lease, since the 1993 Act provides a right to perpetual renewal of leases; and

- the insertion of a requirement for the leaseholder not to grant a sub-lease of the property to a sub-lessee that would last so long as to give the sub-lessee a right by law to buy a new long lease.

Deciding whether to buy a lease extension or enfranchise

When leaseholders are trying to decide whether to buy individual lease extensions or pursue collective enfranchisement, it is important to examine the most pressing issues for residents in the building. Each building has its own dynamic and individual leaseholders have their own priorities and budgets.

Residents are more likely to succeed in enfranchising if they know their neighbours, have a committed team of organisers and live in a building where leases have more than 50 years to run. Before the arrival of email, it was difficult for residents to pull together a strong lobbying group if many leaseholders lived overseas or in other parts of the United Kingdom. But now buildings that have even a large percentage of absentee leaseholders can enfranchise by making effective use of email to rally support for a planned freehold purchase and to keep all leaseholders informed.

When leaseholders have as little as 20 years left on their leases and there is little or no organisational capability displayed by residents, individual lease extensions can represent an attractive option. A lease extension may also be the most logical route if few residents in the building are interested in enfranchising. This can be the case in blocks of flats with many senior citizens that have no relatives, no plans to move and little incentive to increase the market value of their property.

Any resident buying a very short lease must be careful to find out whether the vendor has already started the lease extension process. If the vendor has begun the formal process of getting a lease extension, he should assign this lease-extension right to his buyer. Otherwise, the buyer would have to wait two years before he is able to serve a tenant's notice on the landlord for a lease extension.

In some buildings, an effort by a number of residents to get a group discount on buying lease extensions evolves into an enfranchisement initiative. This is because the cost to each participant of enfranchising is often not much more than the cost of buying a 90-year lease extension, while enfranchisement brings the added benefits of a 999-year lease extension, and full ownership and control of the building.

CHAPTER 6

The right to manage

Studies carried out by successive governments in the United Kingdom have concluded that one of the inherent flaws in the leasehold system is the failure to provide adequate protection for residents against building mismanagement by the landlord. As a result, the Commonhold and Leasehold Reform Act 2002 provided leaseholders with the right to take over collectively the management of their building and to do so by compelling the landlord to hand over this right, without having to prove fault on the part of the landlord. Although the right to manage (RTM) as a consumer trend has taken off more slowly than collective enfranchisement and buying lease extensions, a growing number of leaseholders are now pursuing this route. This chapter describes the process, benefits and costs in gaining RTM, and identifies ways in which to ensure the success of such an initiative.

Gaining RTM

The legislative elements that grant leaseholders RTM over their residential building are contained in Chapter 1 of Part 2 of the 2002 Act. After passage of the Act, some experts expected a flood of RTM cases and were surprised when relatively few leaseholders pursued this new option. The reason was simple. Many residents, after comparing the costs and benefits of enfranchisement, lease extensions and RTM, decided to pursue enfranchisement because of the more wide-sweeping rights they stood to gain at the end of the process.

Although adoption of RTM has been slower than expected, many leaseholders say it can deliver real benefits to residents and at a much lower financial cost than enfranchisement. When residents group together to gain RTM over their building through the statutory route, they must set up a so-called RTM company. By the end of 2004 there were 484 RTM companies in England and Wales. While some of these companies had not yet completed the RTM process, many had done so and had experienced little resistance from the landlord. Indeed, only ten leaseholder groups took their RTM campaign all the way through to a hearing at the Leasehold Valuation Tribunal (LVT) during the period from 2002 to early 2005.

The 2002 Act made it much easier for residents to gain RTM by eliminating an earlier requirement for residents to prove fault on the part of the landlord. In some buildings, residents have used RTM as a first step in the process towards eventually buying the freehold through collective enfranchisement. By gaining RTM, these leaseholders seek to create a disincentive for the landlord to maintain control over the building. The landlord can lose interest in maintaining freehold ownership of a block of flats if his loss of RTM means that he is deprived of commissions or other financial benefits gained through management rights.

Qualifying for RTM

Leaseholders can only compel their landlord to hand over RTM over their building if the leaseholders and the building qualify. Not all residents and buildings are eligible. It is important to find out whether the building and all would-be participants qualify before beginning the formal RTM process.

The building qualification for RTM

A building will be eligible for RTM if:

1. it is a separate residential structure (this can include a building that is adjacent and physically joined to another, but that shares no common parts or common structural services with the adjacent buildings);

2. it has two or more flats held by 'qualifying tenants';

3. at least two-thirds of all flats in the building are held by 'qualifying tenants', that is, tenants whose leases had more than 21 years when the leases were first granted;

4. not more than 25 per cent of the building floor space is for commercial use;

5. the landlord is not a charitable housing trust, a local authority or the Crown;

6. the building is not a converted property of four or fewer units where the landlord or an adult member of the landlord's family resides in one of the units as their only or main home;

7. at least 50 per cent of the flats in the building must participate (If there are only two flats in a building, then both flats must participate.); and

8. RTM has not yet been acquired.

There are some other exemptions that make buildings ineligible for RTM. If leaseholders have questions about this, they should contact the Leasehold Advisory Service. Contact details are provided in Appendix 1, 'Useful contacts'.

The resident qualification for RTM

A resident will qualify for participation in RTM if:

1. he has a 'long lease', that is, the lease had more than 21 years at the time it was granted; or

2. he had a long lease that expired and the resident remained in the building under the provisions of Part 1 of the Landlord and Tenant Act 1954 or Schedule 10 of the Local Government and Housing Act 1989.

All qualifying residents have a legal right to become members of an RTM company, which means in essence becoming a shareholder. The landlord also has the right to become a member, although not at the very beginning. This is explained below.

The main phases of gaining RTM

There are five main phases in the formal process of gaining RTM through the statutory route and there is also important preparatory work that must be done before the formal process can start. These phases are described below.

The preparatory stage

Organisers of an RTM initiative must ensure that their residential building qualifies for RTM and that all would-be participants also qualify. It is at this early stage that the RTM company must be set up and registered with Companies House. It is the RTM company, not individual residents, that gains the RTM over the building and bears the responsibilities that go along with this right. The company can be set up by a minimum of two qualifying residents in the building. It is not necessary at this stage to have the minimum 50 per cent of all flats signed up. An RTM company is a private company limited by guarantee that has a prescribed Memorandum and Articles of Association. This means that all RTM companies must use the government-provided wording for their so-called 'MemArts'. An RTM company cannot use MemArts with whichever wording they choose, including the standard wording for limited companies. A copy of the prescribed MemArts for RTM companies can be obtained from The Stationery Office, contact details of which are in Appendix 1, 'Useful contacts'.

Once the RTM company has been set up, it is a legal requirement that all qualifying residents be invited to become members. The landlord has a right to become a member, but not at this stage. The landlord has a right to become a member only after RTM has been granted to the leaseholders. The leaseholders that are organising the RTM initiative must send the notice of invitation to participate using a prescribed form. This is set out in Statutory Instrument 2003 Number 1988, Landlord and Tenant, England, the Right to Manage (Prescribed Particulars and Forms) (England) Regulations 2003, which is provided in Appendix 9, 'Invitation to participate in right to manage'. The organisers must give all qualifying residents a minimum of 14 days' written notice to become members of the RTM company before the formal RTM process can begin. Once a minimum of 50 per cent of all flats have formally become members of the RTM company, the RTM company is ready to begin the formal process of applying for RTM.

Phase 1: The tenant's RTM claim notice

The formal RTM process begins when the RTM company sends an RTM claim notice to the landlord. This notifies the landlord that the leaseholders are applying for the right to take over management of the building. The RTM company cannot serve the claim notice until it has given a minimum of 14 days' written notice to all qualifying tenants of the notice of invitation to participate. The landlord must be given a minimum of one month by which he must reply to the claim notice. The deadline date must be stated in the claim notice. The claim notice must also specify the date on which the RTM company claims the right to take over management, which must be a date no less than three months after the date on which the counter-notice must be served. By law, a copy of the claim notice must be sent to all qualifying residents in the building on the date on which the claim notice is served on the landlord. The claim notice and other relevant notices may be served by regular postal service, although registered post is recommended. The form for the RTM claim notice is provided in Appendix 10, 'Right to manage notice'.

Phase 2: The landlord's counter-notice

The landlord may serve a counter-notice on the RTM company, although this is not required by law. In the counter-notice, the landlord either admits that the RTM company is entitled to acquire RTM or else he disputes the RTM application. The landlord may only dispute the RTM application on two possible grounds, that the building itself does not qualify for RTM or that the required minimum level of participation of 50 per cent of all flats has not been obtained. The landlord may also wish to use the counter-notice to raise relevant issues about management of the building. The landlord also has the right not to send any counter-notice. If the landlord does not serve a counter-notice on the RTM company, then the RTM company may proceed to take over management of the building. It can commence management of the building a minimum of three months after the deadline date for the landlord to send the counter-notice, that is, a minimum of four months from the date on which the RTM company served the claim notice on the landlord. If the landlord serves a counter-notice disputing the claim and the RTM company takes no further action in the subsequent two months, this is classified as a 'deemed withdrawal' of the RTM company's claim notice. Deemed withdrawals are explained below.

Phase 3: The application to the LVT

If the landlord disputes the claim notice and the RTM company wishes to pursue its claim notice, then the RTM company must make an application to the LVT. The LVT will then make a decision. If an application is made to the LVT by the RTM company, this must be made a maximum of two months from the date on which the counter-notice was served.

Phase 4: The LVT hearing and its decision

The LVT will decide whether the RTM claim notice is valid and thus whether the RTM company has the right to take over management of the building. The LVT may hold a hearing or may simply issue a written decision. It should be noted that there is no need for an RTM company to apply to the LVT in the event that the landlord does not serve a counter-notice or does not contest the RTM claim. Some residents' groups decide to apply to the LVT anyway, even if the landlord serves no counter-notice, to have the LVT's binding decision. If the landlord serves a counter-notice that acknowledges the right of the RTM to take over management of the building, there is no need to apply to the LVT.

Phase 5: Taking over the management of the building

After the LVT has issued a written decision granting the RTM company the right to manage the building, the RTM company will commence management. If the landlord has sent no counter-notice and there has been no LVT involvement, the RTM company may commence management no sooner than three months after the deadline date for the landlord to send the counter-notice. Once the RTM company takes over management of the building, the landlord has a right to become a member of the RTM company. The landlord must, by this stage, provide a list to the RTM company of all contractors with which the landlord has contracts or other agreements regarding the building. The RTM company may wish to continue using these contractors, which can include services such as insurance, cleaning and lift maintenance, but the RTM is not bound to do so. However, it is worth noting that this is a contentious and still largely untested area. It is not yet clear, for instance, whether some landlords will try to pass on to RTM companies possible costs incurred in paying penalty fees for cancelling contracts.

The timeframe of RTM

Although gaining RTM costs less money than buying a lease extension or collectively enfranchising the building, the statutory timeframe means the process can take the better part of a year. This is because the legislation was designed to ensure that each party has sufficient time to respond in writing to the other. The table below shows a best-case schedule for gaining RTM through all five phases, if residents move as rapidly as possible from one phase to the next.

Event	Month in which the event occurs
The tenant's RTM claim notice is served on the landlord by the RTM company	Month 1
The counter-notice is served on the RTM company by the landlord	Month 2
The RTM company applies to the LVT	Month 4
The LVT hearing is held	Month 7
The LVT decision is issued	Month 8

It should be remembered that a vast majority of RTM cases are concluded before an LVT hearing takes place, which means the process lasts only a few months.

The costs involved in gaining RTM

Leaseholders that are pursuing an RTM initiative must bear the cost of setting up the RTM company, in accordance with the Companies Act. An

RTM company, like any company, will then bear various costs as part of its day-to-day operations. These may include book-keeping and accounting, communicating with shareholders, preparing and sending required documentation to Companies House, and preparing and holding Annual General Meetings.

The RTM company must also bear the so-called 'reasonable costs' of the landlord in handling the RTM claim notice. These do not include any costs involved in an LVT hearing. In the event of an LVT hearing, each side bears its own costs. If the RTM company wishes at any stage to challenge whether some or all of the costs claimed by the landlord in handling an RTM claim notice are 'reasonable', it may do so through the nearest LVT.

If a claim notice ceases to have effect, then the RTM company must also bear the reasonable costs incurred by the landlord in having handled the tenant's RTM notice claim, including preparing and serving the counter-notice. A claim notice will cease to have effect if an RTM company goes bankrupt, is wound-up, struck off by Companies House or otherwise ceases to exist. A claim notice will also cease to have effect if it is deemed to have been withdrawn, including where an RTM company fails to apply to the LVT within two months of receiving a counter-notice or other notice disputing the right to take over the management of the building or where the RTM company withdraws an application from the LVT.

If an RTM case goes to the LVT, each side pays its own costs, unless the LVT determines that the RTM company is not eligible to get RTM. However, leaseholders can make an application to the LVT asking that a certain limit be placed on the amount of money that can be recovered.

The rights and responsibilities of the RTM company

An RTM company, once it has gained RTM, is responsible for fulfilling obligations set out in leases held by qualifying residents to maintain and manage the building. It is essential for RTM organisers to read carefully through the lease before embarking on an RTM initiative, in order to be clear about these management and maintenance responsibilities. The responsibilities normally include insurance, cleaning and other services in the building, repairs, maintenance and management of all or part of the building.

If the lease specifies that approval from the landlord must be obtained by long leaseholders before certain activities may be undertaken, including alterations, improvements, subletting and the sale of units, this power to authorise passes to the RTM company once it has gained RTM. The RTM company only has the authority to grant such approvals regarding long-lease flats. The RTM company, before granting any such approvals, must provide a minimum 30 days' written notice to the landlord.

An RTM company is not responsible for maintenance and repairs to the inside of flats that are owned by the landlord.

An RTM company does not have the right to grant lease extensions.

The success factors in gaining RTM

This section identifies some of the issues that come up when leaseholders are seeking to gain RTM and it presents solutions for avoiding pitfalls that can foil an RTM initiative. Several of these issues are illustrated in case study D in Appendix 2, 'Case studies'.

From informal to formal RTM

Many leaseholders, especially in converted houses with a small number of flats, already effectively have RTM because they run their building and get necessary maintenance and repairs done. However, leaseholders should not assume that they have the legal right to take over the management of the building unless they have formally obtained it. Some residents have managed a building for years, only to discover one day that the landlord has handed over management rights to a managing agent without consulting leaseholders. If residents want RTM, it is best to formalise this.

Inviting all leaseholders to participate

It remains best practice for residents, when they enfranchise, to send a formal written invitation to participate to all leaseholders in the building. However, it has not been required by law to do so, according to the Commonhold and Leasehold Reform Act 2002 at the time of writing. RTM is different in this respect. All qualifying leaseholders must by law be sent a written invitation to participate and they must be given a minimum of 14 days to consider this before the formal RTM process begins. Residents are advised to give leaseholders a significantly longer period of time than 14 days, to ensure that leaseholders have adequate time to consider the invitation.

The landlord as an RTM member

Once the RTM company has gained the right to take over the management of the building, the landlord then has a right to become a member of the company. This is understandable since the landlord, as the freeholder, continues to have ownership of the building and thus has an interest in seeing that the property is managed properly.

The right of the RTM company to obtain information

The RTM company has the right to get information from the landlord that is needed for determining how to formulate the tenant's RTM claim notice. The landlord must provide this information within 28 days of receiving a written request.

Ceasing an RTM

If an RTM company ceases to hold management rights for a building, then a new RTM initiative cannot be started for four years, unless the LVT determines that a new RTM initiative can be started sooner than this. The RTM company ceases to have the legally-defined right to management if:

- it wishes to cease to exist and the landlord agrees;

- it is shut down, stuck off by Companies House, enters into receivership or becomes insolvent; or

- it ceases to be an RTM company, for instance, because it is used to purchase the building freehold.

Choosing between DIY management and a managing agent

Many residents are keen to gain RTM in order to ensure that they get value for money when they pay service charges for building management. In some cases, leaseholders that have gained RTM decide to take on the management of the building themselves instead of using an outside managing agent company. While this type of do-it-yourself management may work in some small buildings, including houses that have been converted into flats, leaseholders in large buildings are advised to hire a managing agent. It can often represent a false economy for leaseholders to manage a large building themselves in order to avoid paying a management fee to a managing agent. This is because the one or two dedicated residents that normally carry out this unpaid function are, in effect, subsidising an artificially low service charge for the rest of the leaseholders. Also, residents rarely have the same level of expertise in maintaining and repairing such properties as managing agents. Finally, the departure of one or two dedicated residents that have managed the building for free, by donating their time, can throw a building into chaos when there are no new volunteers to take on this unpaid work.

This issue is examined in case study A in Appendix 2, 'Case studies'.

RTM before collective enfranchisement

Some buildings that tried to enfranchise before the Commonhold and Leasehold Reform Act 2002 came into effect found it a difficult and overly complex process, and their initiatives failed. Many attempted enfranchisements have been foiled over the years by landlords that have fought hard to frustrate residents' attempts to buy the freehold at a fair price within a reasonable amount of time. In some cases, residents that have tried and failed to enfranchise have later turned to the option of RTM, as a phased approach towards eventually buying the freehold. By taking away the landlord's RTM over a building, residents can often make it less attractive for the landlord to continue to hold his freehold interest in the property. This is because many landlords have, through their RTM, earned commissions and enjoyed other financial benefits, for example, by using their own in-house departments or associated companies to provide insurance, cleaning, repairs, maintenance and other services to the building. Some chartered surveyors claim that the cost of the freehold can be lower if residents already have RTM.

Lease extensions and RTM

While gaining RTM costs less money for residents than the options of buying lease extensions or acquiring the freehold, it is important for leaseholders to remember that RTM does not bring with it the right to grant longer leases. If residents gain RTM, they will still need to go to the landlord if and when they want to buy lease extensions. It is for this reason that many residents opt for the 'big bang' solution provided by collective enfranchisement, since buying the freehold delivers the right to extend leases by 999 years, and to own and manage the building.

Deciding whether to pursue RTM or other options

There is no one-size-fits-all solution for every residential building. When considering whether to gain RTM, buy lease extensions, acquire the freehold or stick with the status quo, residents need to consider what are the most pressing issues in the building and what are the resources, in terms of money, time and organisational skills, that are available in order to pursue each possible route.

Residents might decide to gain RTM if their leases have 999 years to run, but where they feel that the landlord is providing an inadequate or overly-expensive management service in the building. Residents that have just 40 years left on their leases and do not wish to work with their neighbours in the building might opt to buy individual lease extensions. Those in a building with 70 years on their leases, a well-established residents' association and a committed team of organisers might decide to pursue collective enfranchisement, with its greater benefits.

Leaseholders need to remember that gaining RTM does not prevent the landlord from seeking to sell the freehold. In this case, the landlord must offer the right of first refusal to the leaseholders. This is explained in chapter 8, 'Buying the freehold through the right of first refusal'.

CHAPTER 7

Going to the Leasehold Valuation Tribunal

Owning leasehold property in England and Wales can be seen as a good-news bad-news story. On the one hand, leaseholders of flats must cope with a system that provides them with far more limited home ownership than equivalent property systems in Europe, the United States and Australia. The bulk of English land law remains woefully antiquated and complex in this regard and it often requires enormous time and effort for leaseholders to achieve even a basic understanding of their rights.

On the other hand, the situation for leaseholders in England and Wales has improved noticeably in recent years. The Leasehold Reform, Housing and Urban Development Act 1993 and the Commonhold and Leasehold Reform Act 2002 equipped leaseholders with important new legal rights. In addition, leaseholders can now turn to the independent body, the Residential Property Tribunal Service (RPTS), which adjudicates in disputes between landlords and residents.

Going to the Leasehold Valuation Tribunal

In recent years thousands of disputes between landlords and residents have been settled by a special tribunal called the Leasehold Valuation Tribunal (LVT), which makes up part of the RPTS. Few leaseholders knew of the existence of the LVT a decade ago, but public awareness is growing as more and more flat owners combine forces to buy the freehold of their building. While many leaseholders and observers say that the LVT system is too unwieldy and slow-moving to ensure adequate protection of flat owners' rights, the LVT has made marked improvements since 2002 in putting in place processes and procedures that are more efficient, transparent and user-friendly.

Between 1994 and 2004, the LVT held 753 hearings regarding leaseholders wanting to buy lease extensions or the freehold of their building. Between 1998 and 2004, there were 1,415 LVT hearings about flat owners challenging the reasonableness of service charges imposed by their landlords. These numbers reveal, however, just the tip of the iceberg regarding the number of cases handled each year at the LVT. This is because a vast majority of applications made by residents to the LVT for a hearing are dropped before the hearing actually takes place. This happens when landlords reach negotiated settlements with residents, a move commonly made by landlords to avoid incurring costs at an LVT hearing.

How the RPTS works

The RPTS has a wide-ranging mandate in resolving disputes regarding everything from building insurance to recognition of residents' associations to deciding on the price of a building freehold when a landlord cannot be found. In recent years the RPTS has made increased efforts to provide transparency to the public regarding its function and structure.

The structure of the RPTS

The RPTS describes its role as providing high-quality, fair and cost-effective adjudication to help landlords, leaseholders and other residents settle disputes about leasehold property and rents. The RPTS says that it aims to provide a tribunal service that is less costly for the parties involved than the court system. The official status of the RPTS is a tribunal non-departmental public body sponsored by the Office of the Deputy Prime Minister. The most senior members of the public-facing committees and tribunals within the RPTS are appointed by the Lord Chancellor, while other adjudicating members in these bodies are appointed by the Office of the Deputy Prime Minister.

The RPTS in England comprises five regional offices, which are called Rent Assessment Panels. Each office covers a different part of the country. There are Rent Assessment Panels for London, Southern England, Northern England, the Midlands and Eastern England. Wales has its own Rent Assessment Panel. A list of these offices is provided in Appendix 1, 'Useful contacts'.

Each Rent Assessment Panel comprises:

- Rent Assessment Committees;

- Rent Tribunals; and

- LVTs.

The structure of the RPTS in England is shown below.

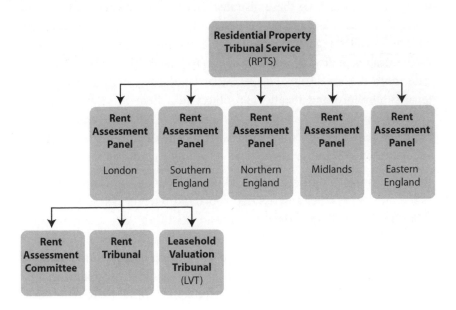

Source of information: Residential Property Tribunal Service

Each Rent Assessment Panel is headed by a President, who is an experienced property lawyer or valuer. The President is supported by one or more Vice-Presidents, who may also be lawyers or valuers. The Presidents and Vice-Presidents are appointed by the Lord Chancellor and work on a part-time basis. The RPTS also has an appointed Senior President, who has overall responsibility for policy and procedures.

Each regional Rent Assessment Panel comprises members who are lawyers, valuers or laypeople. The members, who can work for one or more Panel, are appointed to sit on the committees and tribunals that comprise each Rent Assessment Panel. Members that are allowed to chair tribunals are appointed by the Office of the Deputy Prime Minister. Each Rent Assessment Panel has a Panel Secretary who is responsible for handling correspondence and other documentation, and providing administrative support for the Panel.

Rent Assessment Committees

Rent Assessment Committees deal with disputes over rent paid by tenants living in flats. Many of these disputes concern flats owned by landlords and that are not leasehold properties. Some of these disputes involve rent paid by so-called regulated tenants living in rent-controlled flats. While it is the responsibility of an official body called The Rent Service to determine the maximum fair rent that landlords can charge regulated tenants, landlord and tenants can object to a Rent Service decision by applying to a Rent Assessment Committee. There are relatively few regulated tenancies left since these were mostly established as a result of the Rent Act 1977 and many regulated tenants are now senior citizens.

Rent Assessment Committees also adjudicate rent disputes concerning so-called assured tenants and assured shorthold tenants. These are tenants that also pay rent to the owner of a residential unit. Most people renting flats in London and other parts of England and Wales have assured shorthold tenancies. This includes people renting flats from the landlord or freeholder, and those that sublet from a leaseholder. More information about these tenancies is provided in chapter 10, 'From leasehold to rental'.

Rent Tribunals

Rent Tribunals decide on the maximum amount of rent that should be charged to tenants where the landlord lives in the property and where there is a restricted contract between the resident landlord and the tenant. Landlords, tenants and local authorities can make applications to Rent Tribunals.

LVTs

LVTs have become increasingly busy in recent years because they handle the fastest-growing areas of dispute between landlords and residents. LVTs have the power to:

- decide on the reasonableness of service charges to be paid by leaseholders to the landlord;

- decide on prices to be paid by leaseholders for lease extensions and building freeholds;

- adjudicate in disputes about the right of first refusal, when landlords want to sell their freehold;

- settle disputes over a landlord's choice of insurer;

- decide on leaseholders' requests for the right to manage their building;

- dispense with a landlord's obligation to consult leaseholders on major works when emergency repairs must be done quickly;

- appoint managers to a residential building;

- vary leases; and

- vary estate management schemes.

The LVT hearing

As we discussed in chapter 2, 'Service charge disputes and other grounds for litigation', the LVT processes disputes using the following three-track system:

1. on paper, without a hearing;

2. fast track, with a hearing;

3. standard track, with a hearing and possibly a pre-trial review.

When leaseholders complete the relevant LVT form to send an application to the Tribunal, they are asked to assess whether their application can be handled without a hearing, whether it needs a hearing but is simple enough to follow a fast track procedure or whether it is complex enough to require the slower standard track. Applications sent to the LVT about service charge disputes are often handled purely by written correspondence without a hearing. The purchase of a building freehold requires a hearing. If a case is complex, the Tribunal will hold a pre-trial review, a kind of mini-hearing which is described below.

As we have mentioned, an LVT panel comprises up to three members, a lawyer, a valuer and a layperson. In some cases, there are just two members, with one being a valuer. Some LVT hearings last as little as half a day. This can be the case, for instance, if two leaseholders owning both flats in a converted house wish to buy the freehold, but the landlord is nowhere to be found. Most LVT hearings last one or two days, and some three-day hearings occur in highly contentious cases.

LVT hearings in London are held at the office of the London Rent Assessment Panel. Hearings in the other four regions are sometimes held at the local town hall or can even be held in the home of a tenant, if there is an issue regarding restricted mobility. After the hearing has been held, the Tribunal sends its written decision to both parties.

The LVT pre-trial review

If a case is complex, the LVT will conduct a pre-trial review and this will be conducted by an LVT chairperson, who can conduct the review alone or with one or two members. At the pre-trial review the chairperson may wish to examine the application and documentation sent by either party, to find out whether some aspects of the case can be settled and to decide on any steps to be taken before the hearing. Next steps will often include directing either or both parties to provide specific documentation and sending this to the LVT and to the other party.

Pre-trial reviews are held in order to identify issues and establish the way forward, and are not used for deciding on issues in the case. The review establishes the procedure for calling expert witnesses, preparing and exchanging documentation, and doing other work in the run-up to the hearing.

The RPTS says that the LVT gives both parties at least 21 days' notice of the date on which a pre-trial review will be held.

LVT inspections

The RPTS says that LVT panels and Rent Assessment Committees seek to visit properties that are the subject of hearings. This inspection of the inside of the property is arranged only if the permission of the resident has been obtained. Such inspections are usually carried out on the day of the hearing, but they can also be done before or after the hearing date. LVTs sometimes also wish to visit other similar properties and/or walk around the immediate neighbourhood, including if the hearing concerns a collective enfranchisement.

Costs at the LVT

The cost of filing an application at the LVT varies from £50 to £350, depending on the size of the building, the number of residential units and, if relevant, the amount of money being disputed. It costs, for instance, £50 for a leaseholder to file an LVT application that challenges the reasonableness of service charges amounting to £500 or less. If the disputed service charges total more than £15,000, the application fee is £350. The tables below provide information on the cost of application fees for service charge disputes, requests to vary leases and landlord requests to dispense with requirements to consult leaseholders on major works, when emergency repairs need to be carried out.

Challenging the Reasonableness of Service Charges
Form S27A Landlord and Tenant Act 1985

Amount of service charges in dispute	Application fee
Not more than £500	£50
More than £500 but less than £1,000	£70
More than £1,000 but less than £5,000	£100
More than £5,000 but less than £15,000	£200
More than £15,000	£350

Request to Vary (Change) a Lease

Form Part IV Landlord and Tenant Act 1987

Amount of service charges in dispute	Application fee
Five or fewer dwellings	£150
Between six and ten dwellings	£250
More than ten dwellings	£350

Request by Landlord for Dispensation of Consultation Requirements

Form 20ZA Landlord and Tenant Act 1985

Number of dwellings in which application relates	Application fee
Five or fewer dwellings	£150
Between six and ten dwellings	£250
More than ten dwellings	£350

As a general rule, each party pays its own way regarding the cost of any solicitor, surveyor or barrister instructed to appear at an LVT hearing. As we have seen, it is because of this that the vast majority of landlords settle collective enfranchisement and lease extensions cases before an LVT hearing is held, since they want to avoid paying any LVT costs.

Some leases state that a landlord may seek to recover from tenants some or all of the costs that are incurred at a court or tribunal hearing and that the landlord may do so by incorporating these costs into the building service charges. Section 20C of the Landlord and Tenant Act 1985, however, gives the Tribunal the power, if requested by the tenant, to make an order that prevents the landlord from taking such a step. In order to ensure that the landlord is not able to recover any LVT costs from the tenant, the tenant needs to complete and send to the LVT an S20C Application Form.

The change in customer focus

Before the passage of the Commonhold and Leasehold Reform Act 2002, many residents complained that the LVT process was painfully slow. Indeed, some enfranchisement cases took years. Since then, the RPTS has sought to create more efficiency in processing what is often an enormous amount of applications.

The RPTS says that its Rent Assessment Panels now aim to deal with 90 per cent of disputes about rent within a maximum of ten weeks of receiving written applications. For disputes concerning leasehold property, including collective enfranchisements and lease extensions, the Panels seek to schedule an LVT hearing within a maximum of 20 weeks of receiving the initial written application.

Some LVT staff members say that the Tribunals are operationally equipped to schedule hearings even more quickly, but that landlords have said this would not provide them with adequate time to carry out the work they need to do to prepare for an LVT hearing.

Rent Assessment Panels have a publicly-stated target to send written decisions to the relevant parties within four weeks of Rent Assessment Committee hearings that are held on rent disputes and within six weeks of LVT hearings on leasehold cases.

The limits to LVT power

The existence of the LVT is undoubtedly making a difference for residents who want to buy a lease extension or their building freehold, to secure the right to manage or to exercise other legal rights. However, it is important to note that LVTs have limited power when it comes to certain financial aspects of a dispute between a landlord and a resident.

As we discussed in chapter 2, 'Service charge disputes and other grounds for litigation', for instance, if leaseholders in a building challenge the reasonableness of service charges that they have already paid, then, even if the LVT decides in their favour, they will still need to file a claim in the County court later on to get the court to order the landlord to reimburse them. This is because the LVT, as a quasi-judicial body, does not have the same enforcement power as a court.

The deterrent power of the LVT

We have discussed the fact that very few of the applications made to the LVT by leaseholders result in LVT hearings. In the case of enfranchisement, this is because landlords look to avoid paying a solicitor, surveyor and possibly barrister at a hearing by reaching a negotiated settlement with the residents before the hearing. Such negotiated settlements are often concluded in the days leading up to the scheduled LVT hearing.

The labour-intensive processing of LVT applications and hearing schedules, only for the hearings to be cancelled at the last minute, is a source of some frustration for LVT staff. However, it is clear that the very existence of the LVT has acted as a strong deterrent in recent years against some of the more extreme types of abuse by landlords of residents' rights that were common in many buildings up through the 1990s.

Sadly, few leaseholders are aware that it is unusual for enfranchisement or lease extension cases to go all the way to an LVT hearing. Many residents are discouraged from pursuing the statutory route to buy a lease extension or their building freehold because they believe mistakenly that all such cases go to an LVT hearing and that they will have to pay a solicitor, surveyor and/or barrister to represent them.

Appealing against LVT decisions

Before the Commonhold and Leasehold Reform Act 2002, landlords appealed against a large number of LVT decisions to the Lands Tribunal. However, the regulations have changed and now either party can appeal an LVT decision only after receiving written permission from the LVT or the Lands Tribunal. The rules were changed as a result of what was seen as an abuse of the system by freeholders, including some of England's biggest landlords.

If either party wishes to appeal against an LVT decision, this must be done within 28 days of the LVT decision.

Obtaining more information

The website of the RPTS, located at www.rpts.gov.uk, has plentiful information about the role of the LVT and Rent Assessment Committees. It also has downloadable forms for making applications to the LVT. Leaseholders can also obtain information on the LVT process and related issues by contacting the Leasehold Advisory Service. Contact information is provided in Appendix 1, 'Useful contacts'.

CHAPTER 8

Buying the freehold through the right of first refusal

Many residents of flats in England and Wales have the right to be offered the opportunity to buy their building if the landlord wishes to sell. An increasing number of blocks of flats and converted houses are being purchased by leaseholders and other residents through this right of first refusal process. According to the law, if a landlord in such a case sells a building to a third party without first providing the right of first refusal to leaseholders, he commits a criminal offence. While some residents are aware of their rights in this area, a large number are caught off guard when they receive an official right of first refusal notice from the landlord, which presents a tight deadline by which they must reply. This chapter describes the phases and costs involved in buying a freehold through the right of first refusal, and provides important information for ensuring the success of such an acquisition.

The right of first refusal

For decades, leaseholders have complained to government and local authorities about a failure by many landlords to communicate in a responsible manner with residents in the building, including about important issues regarding building management and repairs. In a large number of cases, residents have been unable even to identify or locate the landlord. Others have experienced the unpleasant shock of learning that the landlord has sold the freehold of the building to a third party without first consulting residents.

These problems led years ago to changes in the law that included creating a legal requirement for landlords to offer a building with flats to its leaseholders and other qualifying residents before selling to a third party. The law that first provided this right of first refusal was the Landlord and Tenant Act 1987. This legislation was subsequently amended by the Housing Act 1996.

The right of first refusal applies whether the landlord wishes to sell the freehold to a known third party or at auction. Leaseholders are placed at a certain disadvantage when buying through the right of first refusal, as compared to collective enfranchisement, since they are presented with a sale price and have no legal right to negotiate on the price. Residents also need to move swiftly under a tighter set of deadlines when the landlord serves a right of first refusal notice, since, unlike enfranchisement, they are not the ones organising the freehold purchase process and deciding when to serve notice on the landlord. Despite these disadvantages, many residents decide to buy through the right of first refusal if they have determined that the landlord has asked a fair price. On the landlords' side, a growing number are opting to sell their buildings through the right of first refusal process in order to avoid being caught by surprise by enfranchisement initiatives.

Issues regarding the right of first refusal are illustrated in case study C in Appendix 2, 'Case studies'.

Qualifying for the right of first refusal

In order for residents to buy the property in which they live or own flats through a right of first refusal process, both the property and the participating residents must qualify. A landlord should be aware of whether residents are eligible for the right of first refusal.

The building qualification for the right of first refusal

The right of first refusal can apply to all or part of a building. The right will apply to a property if:

1.   it contains two or more flats held by 'qualifying tenants';

2. more than 50 per cent of the flats in the property are held by qualifying tenants;

3. not more than 50 per cent of the property's internal floor space is for commercial use, not counting common parts such as staircases, landings, lobbies and hallways;

4. more than 50 per cent of the qualifying tenants are participating in the purchase of the freehold;

5. the landlord is not a charitable housing trust, a local authority or the Crown;

6. the building is not a house converted into flats in which the landlord occupies one of the flats as his only or main home and has done so for at least 12 months before the beginning of the freehold sale process.

There are other exemptions regarding buildings in which residents do not have a right of first refusal. If you are in doubt, you should contact the Leasehold Advisory Service. Contact details are provided in Appendix 1, 'Useful contacts'.

The resident qualification for the right of first refusal

A resident will have a right of first refusal if:

1. he has a 'long lease', that is, the lease had more than 21 years at the time it was granted, or the resident is a 'regulated tenant';

2. he does not own or have a tenancy of more than two flats in the building;

3. he is not a 'protected shorthold tenant', an 'assured tenant', an agricultural-occupancy tenant, a business tenant, a resident subletting from a leaseholder or a resident with a tenancy that terminates upon the cessation of employment.

Regulated tenancy and other non-leasehold tenancies

Regulated tenants, or protected tenants as they are also called, are residents that rent their flats directly from the landlord and that do so under a scheme that protects them against eviction and certain increases in rent. These rent-protected tenancies date back mostly to the Rent Act 1977. Regulated tenancies normally cover tenancy agreements that were reached before January 1989. Because regulated tenancies are no longer being created and because they apply to long-standing residents, most regulated tenants are senior citizens.

Assured tenancies and protected shorthold tenancies, which have existed since the late 1980s, provide residents with less protection against eviction and rent increases than regulated tenancies. Most people renting flats in England and Wales, whether directly from the landlord or from a leaseholder, have shorthold tenancies.

Regulated tenancies, assured tenancies and protected shorthold tenancies are revisited in chapter 10, 'From leasehold to rental'.

Exceptions to the right of first refusal

There are some instances in which the right of first refusal does not apply to the sale of a building containing flats. These exemptions include transfers within a family trust and sales made as a result of bankruptcy, divorce and compulsory purchase. They also include the transfer of a building freehold by the landlord to an associated company, such as a subsidiary company, as long as the associated company has had this associated status for at least two years.

The main phases of buying the freehold through the right of first refusal

There are four main phases in the process of selling or buying a building by the right of first refusal. These are described below.

Phase 1: The right of first refusal notice

The process begins when the landlord serves a formal notice on the residents that he wishes to sell the property to a third party and is providing a right of first refusal for residents to buy. This is called a Section

5 Notice, because of the relevant part of the law concerned, but we will refer to this as the right of first refusal notice. The landlord must serve the notice in writing on a minimum of 90 per cent of the qualifying tenants in the property or else on at least every qualifying tenant less one, if the building has fewer than ten qualifying tenants.

The notice must identify the property that is to be sold and it must state the sale price. The document must also say that the landlord is offering to provide a contract of sale to qualifying tenants following the stated sale terms. By law, more than 50 per cent of qualifying tenants must accept the sale offer and they must inform the landlord of this in writing within two months of the service of the landlord's notice. This two-month period is known as the initial period in a right of first refusal process. The landlord's notice must identify the date on which the initial period ends, that is, the deadline date, and must state that more than 50 per cent of qualifying tenants must participate in the freehold purchase.

The landlord's notice must also identify a deadline at least two months after the end of the initial period by which the residents must advise the landlord of the identity of a nominee purchaser that will buy the building freehold on their behalf. As we saw in chapter 3, 'Buying the freehold', the nominee purchaser is the legal entity that makes the acquisition. It is usually a limited company formed by the participating residents and of which they are shareholders.

If the landlord serves the right of first refusal notice on different residents on different dates, then the notice will take effect on the latest of these dates.

Phase 2: The residents' notice of acceptance

If more than 50 per cent of the qualifying residents in a building wish to buy the freehold at the price identified by the landlord, then they must communicate this in writing within the two-month initial period, as identified in the landlord's right of first refusal notice. For the purpose of this description, we will refer to this as the 'residents' notice of acceptance'. For the purpose of gathering the required number of more than 50 per cent, the flat of each qualifying resident gets one vote. If the landlord and the qualifying tenants wish to agree that the tenants will be provided with a longer initial period than two months, both parties can agree to this and identify a new later deadline.

If fewer than 50 per cent of the qualifying residents in a building wish to buy the freehold at the landlord's asking price, then the landlord has the right for a period of 12 months to sell the freehold to a third party at the same price. The landlord is not allowed to sell the freehold to a third party at a lower price. If the landlord wishes to drop the price, then he must begin the right of first refusal process again, at the new lower price. This regulation is meant to prevent landlords from offering freeholds to residents at an artificially-high price that they cannot afford, only to sell later at a lower price to a preferred outside buyer.

Phase 3: The notice of nominee purchaser

After participating residents have served the residents' notice of acceptance on the landlord, they then have a maximum period of two months during which they must advise the landlord in writing of the identity of the nominee purchaser that will buy the freehold on their behalf. The nominee purchaser can be a company, one to four individuals, an association or some another entity. Once the participating residents notify the landlord in writing that they have nominated the nominee purchaser to buy the freehold and to act on their behalf in this regard, the landlord will usually communicate only with the nominee purchaser in completing the freehold purchase process. Once the freehold has been acquired, the nominee purchaser becomes the new landlord.

Phase 4: The completion of the freehold purchase

As soon as the participating tenants have sent the notice of nominee purchaser to the landlord, the landlord must send the nominee purchaser a sale contract within a maximum of one month.

Within a maximum of two months of the receipt by the nominee purchaser of the sale contract, the nominee purchaser must return to the landlord the signed contract and a deposit for the building freehold. The deposit must be for an amount that is not more than ten per cent of the total agreed price. If the landlord and the nominee purchaser wish to agree that the nominee purchaser can have more than two months to send back the signed contract and deposit, they may agree to this new later deadline.

Upon receipt of the contract signed by the nominee purchaser, the landlord has a maximum of seven days to exchange contracts or else to withdraw from the sale process. Completion of the freehold purchase then follows the exchange of contracts, as set out in the contract.

The main phases of the right of first refusal for auction sale

If the landlord wishes to sell the building freehold at auction, residents will in most cases also have a right of first refusal. If the residents wish to buy the freehold, their nominee purchaser will basically take the place of the successful bidder at the auction. The main phases for this auction-driven right of first refusal are described below.

Phase 1: The right of first refusal notice for auction sale

The first thing that the landlord must do is to serve a notice on a minimum of 90 per cent of the qualifying tenants in the property or else on at least every qualifying tenant less one, if the building has fewer than ten qualifying tenants. We will refer to this as the right of first refusal notice for auction sale. The landlord must serve this notice between four and six months before the auction. The notice must identify the property to be sold and state the expected sales price. The document must also say that the landlord is planning to sell the freehold at a public auction, and it must identify the deadline at the end of the two-month initial period by which residents must send their written acceptance to buy the freehold. As with a non-auction sale, the notice must state that more than 50 per cent of qualifying tenants must participate in the freehold purchase.

The landlord's right of first refusal notice for auction sale must also identify a further period of at least 28 days from the end of the initial period for participating residents to identify in writing the nominee purchaser. The initial period must end at least two months before the auction and the further period must end at least 28 days before the auction. The landlord must notify residents of the time and place of the auction either in the right of first refusal notice for auction sale or by separate written notice at least 28 days before the auction.

Phase 2: The residents' notice of acceptance

If more than 50 per cent of the qualifying residents want to buy the freehold at the eventual auction price, then they must advise the landlord in writing. They must send this residents' notice of acceptance within the two-month initial period, as identified in the landlord's notice. If the landlord and the qualifying residents want to agree that residents will get a longer initial period than two months, they may do so and identify a new later deadline.

Phase 3: The notice of nominee purchaser

After participating residents have served the residents' notice of acceptance on the landlord, they have a maximum period of 28 days during which to advise the landlord of the identity of their nominee purchaser.

Phase 4: The auction and completion of the freehold purchase

If the building freehold is sold at auction and the landlord agrees a conditional contract with the successful bidder, the landlord must send a copy of the contract to the nominee purchaser within a maximum of seven days of the auction.

The nominee purchaser then has a maximum of 28 days in which to accept the sales price identified in the contract and to fulfil any conditions stated in the contract, including paying a deposit. The contract will then have effect as if the nominee purchaser, and not the successful bidder, had entered into it with the landlord.

Completion of the freehold sale cannot be less than 28 days after the acceptance of the contract by the nominee purchaser.

The timeframe of buying the freehold through the right of first refusal

For residents who are keen to buy their freehold and who feel that the landlord has asked a fair price, right of first refusal offers an advantage of moving the process along more quickly and in a less complex manner than collective enfranchisement. The table below presents a best-case timeframe, if the landlord and participating residents move from one phase of the process to the next at the earliest opportunity allowed by the legislation.

Event	Month in which the event occurs
The landlord serves the right of first refusal notice on the residents	Month 1
The residents' notice of acceptance is served on the landlord	Month 3
The residents serve notice of nominee purchaser on the landlord	Month 5
The landlord sends the sale contract to the nominee purchaser	Month 6
The nominee purchaser sends the signed contract and deposit to the landlord	Month 8
The exchange of contracts by the landlord and the nominee purchaser	Month 8 + 7 days

The timeframe of buying the freehold at auction

The process follows a slightly different timeframe if the landlord plans to sell the building freehold at auction. The table below illustrates a minimum timeframe made possible by law for the right of first refusal for auction sales.

Event	Month in which the event occurs
The landlord serves the right of first refusal notice for auction sale on the residents	Month 1
The residents' notice of acceptance is served on the landlord	Month 3
The residents serve notice of nominee purchaser on the landlord	Month 4
The auction is held; the conditional contract is prepared for the successful bidder	Month 5
The landlord sends the conditional contract to the nominee purchaser	Month 5 + 7 days
The nominee purchaser accepts the contract	Month 6
The exchange of contracts by the landlord and the nominee purchaser	Month 7

The costs involved in the freehold purchase through the right of first refusal

If residents buy their building freehold through the right of first refusal, they pay their own legal and surveyor fees, but, unlike collective enfranchisement, they do not pay the landlord's legal and surveyor fees. This is because buying through the right of first refusal is not a compulsory purchase, so the law says that landlords must pay their own professional fees. The landlord might incorporate his legal and surveyor fees within the freehold price contained in the initial notice, however, and residents do not have a legal right to negotiate on this price.

Both the landlord and the group of participating residents have a right to withdraw from the process of selling or buying the freehold at any stage during the right of first refusal process. Any such withdrawal incurs certain costs for the withdrawing party. Also, if either party fails to meet a statutory deadline or does anything else that is deemed a withdrawal, it will incur withdrawal costs. This is explained below.

Withdrawal from the process

Both parties have the right to withdraw any time before the completion of the freehold sale. If either party wishes to withdraw, it does so by informing the other party in writing. A failure to proceed to the next required phase in the process is also considered a withdrawal. Withdrawal has different implications for each party, depending on which party withdraws.

Withdrawal by residents

If leaseholders serve a residents' notice of acceptance on the landlord and then later withdraw from the process, the landlord has the right for a period of 12 months to sell the building freehold to a third party. The landlord cannot, however, sell the freehold for a lower price than initially offered to the residents. If the landlord does sell the freehold to a third party at a lower price, he commits a criminal offence.

If leaseholders serve a residents' notice of acceptance for auction sale on the landlord and then subsequently withdraw from the process, the landlord has a right for a period of 12 months to sell the freehold at auction, without sending any further notification about this to the residents. If the landlord announces to residents that he intends to sell at auction and then sells the freehold privately, in a non-auction sale, he commits a criminal offence.

If the number of participating residents that wish to buy the freehold falls below the required minimum level of more than 50 per cent of all qualifying tenants, then the nominee purchaser must on behalf of the residents send a notice to the landlord stating that the nominee purchaser is withdrawing.

Withdrawal by the landlord

The landlord may also withdraw from the right of first refusal process of selling the freehold at any stage before completion of the sale. If he withdraws, he may not sell the freehold to a third party until he begins the right of first refusal process again.

Deemed withdrawals

If either party misses a statutory deadline, this is considered a 'deemed withdrawal'. If residents do not send to the landlord the residents' notice of acceptance or the notice of nominee purchaser by the required deadlines, this is a deemed withdrawal. It is also a deemed withdrawal if the nominee purchaser fails to return to the landlord the signed contract and deposit by the relevant deadline.

If a landlord does not send a contract of sale to the nominee purchaser or does not exchange contracts with the nominee purchaser by the required deadlines, this is a deemed withdrawal. In the case of a sale by auction, it is also a deemed withdrawal if the landlord does not proceed with the auction.

The costs of withdrawal

If either party withdraws from the process, then the other party can recover its legal and surveyor costs for the period beginning four weeks after the end of the initial period until the time of the withdrawal.

If the nominee purchaser withdraws from the process, then the landlord can recover costs from the nominee purchaser.

Non-compliance by landlords

If a landlord fails to comply with the right of first refusal procedure and sells a building freehold without offering residents the right of first refusal, he commits a criminal offence. It is also a criminal offence if the landlord sells to a third party for a lower price than the price that was previously rejected by residents through a right of first refusal. These offences are punishable by what is called a 'level 5 fine', which carries a maximum fine of £5,000.

If the landlord sells the freehold to a third party without offering the right of first refusal to qualifying residents, the residents will normally have the right to buy the property from the buyer at the price he paid. The purchaser of the freehold must notify residents in writing after buying the property and must notify them of their right of first refusal. A failure to do this is a criminal offence that carries a level 4 fine of a maximum £2,500.

Deciding to enfranchise when offered the right of first refusal

In many cases, residents are caught by surprise when served a right of first refusal notice and they must act quickly to decide whether they want to buy the freehold. However, in some instances, residents have been considering buying the building and have carried out preparatory work including having a chartered surveyor prepare a valuation report of the freehold.

Depending on the priorities of the residents, their level of preparedness and their available budget and organisational skills, buying the freehold through the right of first refusal may or may not represent the best way forward. The table below identifies the advantages and disadvantages of buying the freehold through the right of first refusal as compared to collective enfranchisement.

Comparing the freehold purchase by the right of first refusal and enfranchisement

	Freehold purchase through collective enfranchisement	Freehold purchase through the right of first refusal
Faster, simpler process for buying the freehold		✔
Residents do not normally pay the landlord's legal and surveyor fees		✔
Residents have the legal right to negotiate the price	✔	

Residents have the legal right to secure a 'fair price' at the Leasehold Valuation Tribunal	✔	

As the table shows, buying through the right of first refusal is a simpler process and often faster than enfranchisement, since there is no debate over the offer and counter-offer prices, and since the Leasehold Valuation Tribunal (LVT) is not normally involved. If residents are confident that the landlord has stated a fair price in a right of first refusal notice, there may be an advantage to buying in this manner.

However, if residents do not believe the landlord has stated a fair price and if they are willing to bear the costs – in terms of money, time and effort – of collectively enfranchising the building, then this process might ensure a better outcome. In the right of first refusal scenario, it is the landlord essentially who controls the process from the start. With a collective enfranchisement, residents have more control over the pace of the process and the manner in which the final price is decided. In some buildings, residents may decide that the higher legal and surveyor fees involved in an enfranchisement represent a worthwhile investment given the expectation that the residents will secure a lower freehold price.

CHAPTER 9

Residents' associations and resident management companies

The basic unit representing the interests of residents in many blocks of flats is the residents' association. These volunteer groups can address a wide variety of issues, from campaigning for improved management of the building to setting up a Neighbourhood Watch team or buying plants to beautify the building's main entrance. As legislative changes have given leaseholders new rights to buy their freehold, acquire lease extensions and gain the right to manage, the residents' association has become an increasingly important vehicle for gathering support amongst leaseholders and other tenants, developing consensus and bringing about lasting changes within a residential building. This chapter examines best practice in setting up and running a residents' association and identifies ways in which to avoid the pitfalls that cause many such volunteer organisations to collapse. At the end of the chapter, we examine the resident management company (RMC) and the ways in which this entity differs from the residents' association.

The evolution of the residents' association

For many years residents' associations in the United Kingdom had limited power to bring about real change in a building. Indeed, until the early

1990s a main point of leverage these groups had over landlords was the ability for members to refuse to pay their service charges. For reasons we shall discuss below, this type of rent strike often proved counterproductive for residents and indeed led to the collapse of many associations. The situation changed dramatically, however, when the Leasehold Reform, Housing and Urban Development Act 1993 gave leaseholders of flats the right to collectively enfranchise. When leaseholders gained this new right to compel the landlord to sell them the freehold of their building, residents' associations took on a more powerful role.

There are thousands of residents' associations across England and Wales. Some associations in large blocks of flats have more than 100 members, while those in a house converted into flats can have as few as two. During the three-year period to December 2004, nearly 2,500 residents' associations applied to the Residential Property Tribunal Service (RPTS) for so-called official recognition, a process that we examine in this chapter. The Federation of Private Residents' Associations (also known as FPRA), the most widely-recognised umbrella group for such organisations, has seen the number of member groups leap from about 200 to 600 in recent years.

While many residents' associations are run by volunteer members in an efficient, fair and accountable manner, there is unfortunately a number of complaints every year about associations in which committee members fail to consult residents properly, abuse their power and even misappropriate funds. This chapter examines ways in which to avoid these problems. We will also look at important changes that result when leaseholders buy the freehold of their building and the residents' association is replaced by a collectively-owned RMC that becomes the new landlord.

Setting up the committee

The committee of a residents' association is the group's decision-making body. Its officers, normally including a chairperson, secretary and treasurer, are elected by association members. Until the 1990s committees of residents' associations in many London mansion blocks represented homogenous groups. Committee members were commonly retired residents that lived full-time in the building. But in recent years, many buildings have sought committees that match the diversity of residents in order best to represent everyone in the building.

It is essential for the head of the residents' association to have strong leadership skills, including the ability to build a competent and effective committee. The head of the association needs well-developed organisational and communication skills, in order to hold together the community of residents from a range of backgrounds and age groups. When residents want to buy the freehold of their building, they will need a chairperson with a known track record for commitment, tenacity and 'lift-off' power. It is ideal if committee members can also bring strong commercial, legal and accountancy expertise to the residents' association.

It can be tempting, when volunteering to head a residents' association, to build a committee of like-minded friends. But these committees, like any effective board of directors, need to avoid the temptation to appoint 'yes men' and 'yes women'. It is essential for committee members to be independent-minded and willing to question, and to avoid engaging in 'group thinking'.

When a new association is being set up, it is acceptable for a committee to be created on an informal volunteer basis. However, all committee members, including the head of the association, should stand for election by members at every annual general meeting (AGM) or else stand for election in rotation, as specified in the association's constitution.

Best practice for residents' associations

Complaints emerge too frequently about residents' association committees that fail to be accountable to members and that misuse power. Some members claim that a significant minority of those volunteering to serve on these committees apply a lower standard for professionalism and financial propriety than they would normally apply to salaried positions in the business world. Residents need to take care to elect only those members that are likely to bring the most professional approach to the work of the committee, which has a serious duty of trust to serve residents.

Residents' associations are bound by few specific legal requirements regarding the creation and running of the organisation, but they should nonetheless be run in a business-like manner that follows best practice in corporate governance, financial transparency, and accountability to members and other major stakeholders.

The constitution

One of the first steps involved in setting up a residents' association, after forming the committee, is to draft and agree a constitution. There is no statutory prescribed constitution for residents' associations. A sample constitution is provided in Appendix 11. The constitution should make clear any rules about membership, membership fees, AGMs, other general meetings, elections of committee members and voting rights.

The AGM

Committee members of large residents' associations often groan when it is time to prepare documentation for the AGM. This is because it can take many hours to prepare such AGM documentation. Documents for an upcoming AGM need to be delivered or sent to every association member and this must be done a specified minimum number of days before the AGM, as stated in the constitution. The documents should include:

- a formal notice of the date, time and venue of the upcoming AGM;
- a profit and loss account for the past year, compared to the year earlier;
- a balance sheet;
- a report from the chairperson;
- an explanation of any special resolutions on which members will vote;
- an absentee ballot form, including for appointing a proxy;
- a copy of the minutes of the previous AGM.

The documents may also contain, if desired, a brief biographical description of committee members or those standing for election. It is also best practice to include in the pre-AGM documentation an invitation to any member to stand for election to the committee. Anyone wishing to stand for election should be nominated and seconded by named individuals.

Some committee members get discouraged when few people show up for the AGM. A failure to attend an AGM should not be interpreted as a lack of interest amongst members. It is common, for instance, for only a tiny minority of shareholders to attend AGMs of publicly-traded companies; despite this, well-run companies take very seriously the importance of giving shareholders this chance once a year to raise questions and to express their views directly to the board of directors.

Electing committee members

Committee members of many residents' associations stand for election or re-election at every AGM. Alternatively, the constitution may state that a required minimum number of committee members resign and stand for re-election at each AGM. The constitution may state that there can be a maximum number of committee members at any one time.

To ensure that the committee is able to do its job and given the fact that people come and go in a block of flats, it is advisable to state in the constitution that the committee has the authority to appoint one or more committee members in between AGMs. These members should subsequently stand for election at the next AGM.

It is not unusual to hear grumbling complaints amongst residents attending an AGM when elections are held in a manner that does not follow proper procedure. Committee members should be elected or re-elected one at a time, with votes requested for those in favour, those against and those abstaining. A written record of the number of votes should be kept. Many residents' associations do a simple hand count at the AGM and these votes need to be added to the votes made by absentee ballot by leaseholders that live elsewhere in the UK, overseas or that otherwise could not attend the AGM. A process by which an entire committee is elected or re-elected in one show of hands is not best practice. It can create resentment amongst association members and can result in accusations of improper procedure.

The membership fee

It is essential for a well-run residents' association to charge an annual membership fee. The annual fee can be a nominal amount such as £10 or

£20 per member. Charging a membership fee is important for several reasons. Firstly, committee members often volunteer a lot of time to do the work of the association, but it is unreasonable to expect that they will spend their own money to cover association costs. Membership fees should be used to cover costs such as the rental of a venue for the AGM, and paper, envelopes and postage when sending AGM documentation to members.

It is also important to charge a membership fee as part of good corporate governance. Some residents' associations have a policy of declaring that every leaseholder in a building is automatically a member of the association and that no membership fee is charged. This is not best practice. Residents should only be described as members of the association if they have expressed the desire verbally or in writing to join. The Rent Assessment Panels of the RPTS look at whether a residents' association charges a membership fee, when deciding whether to grant official recognition, an issue that is explained below.

Some residents' associations choose to provide a discounted membership fee for senior citizens.

Absentee leaseholders

Until the 1990s, many residents' associations despaired when faced with a large number of absentee leaseholders in a building. While it is relatively easy to put a note through every resident's door about an upcoming meeting or other important issue, contacting leaseholders that live in a different part of the United Kingdom or overseas requires extra time, effort and cost.

The arrival of email changed all this by making it much easier to keep the members of a residents' group informed, including those living on the other side of the world. In fact, the existence of absentee leaseholders has recently increased the possibilities for change in many buildings, including when collective enfranchisement is being considered. Because most buy-to-let investors consider their flats purely as financial investments, many of these absentee members of a residents' association will sign up quickly to join a project to buy the freehold of the building.

The existence of absentee leaseholders used to make it difficult to collectively enfranchise a building. Under the Leasehold Reform, Housing and Urban Development Act 1993, at least half of all participants in an enfranchisement had to live full-time in the building. This residency requirement was eliminated, however, with the Commonhold and Leasehold Reform Act 2002.

Residents' associations should expect a rise in the number of absentee leaseholders, as buy-to-let investments increase and growing prosperity prompts many households to own a flat in London and a house in the English countryside. Association committees need to keep updated lists of all members and should also keep a list of non-member residents. If knocking on doors fails to provide names and contact information, an online search of leaseholders' titles at HM Land Registry at www.land registeronline.gov.uk will at least provide the name of leaseholders.

Having several absentee leaseholders can help create a more efficient communications system for the association committee, since residents cannot simply be updated on important events when meeting in the hallway or lift. Committee members in large buildings should avoid answering every email query as soon as it arrives, in order to avoid creating an impression that committee members work full-time for the association. It is better to send regular update notes to members, including when there is a major milestone in a project such as buying the building freehold.

Non-leaseholder membership

Some residents' associations follow a practice of only allowing members that are long leaseholders, that is, whose leases had more than 21 years when first granted. Other residents, including regulated tenants, who rent flats directly from the landlord, and subtenants, who rent from leaseholders, are excluded from membership. Many associations allow only long leaseholders as members because these are the residents who pay the service charges and thus they have specific rights by law that other residents do not have, such as being consulted by the landlord on major repairs and on other work paid for by service charges. The RPTS strongly encourages the creation of leaseholder-only residents' associations.

The exclusion of non-leaseholders from residents' associations is not a welcome trend. In many buildings it has created unnecessary divisions amongst residents. It has also isolated some of the most vulnerable residents, including senior citizens that are regulated tenants, and has denied them badly-needed protection by residents' associations.

It is best practice for residents' associations to invite all the residents in a building to join, whether they are leaseholders, regulated tenants, sub-lessees or others. However, the constitution must make clear that the only members that are allowed to vote on matters relating to service charges are those that pay service charges. This policy ensures, for instance, that only those residents that will be paying for a new intercom system will be allowed to vote on whether to buy the new system. The constitution must also make clear that there is only one vote per flat and that a vote by a leaseholder takes precedence over a vote by a sub-lessee of the same flat.

With the growth in buy-to-let investment, it is easy for an 'us against them' social division to emerge in a building between leaseholders and sub-lessees. It is important for residents' associations to help develop a sense of community and mutual responsibility amongst everyone in the building, whether leaseholder, sub-lessee or regulated tenant.

Corporate governance and handling money

There have been some alarming cases of residents' association funds being embezzled by committee members, but these rarely make newspaper headlines since the theft is on a smaller scale than in many instances of corporate fraud. Committee members have a responsibility to put in place processes and procedures that minimise the possibility that funds will be wittingly or unwittingly misused. It is best practice, for instance, for the signatures of two committee members to be required on all cheques drawn on the association bank account. When a committee member is seeking the counter-signature of another committee member on a cheque, an invoice or other explanatory documentation should be attached to the cheque.

Awkward moments can occur at AGMs of residents' associations when one or more members raise questions about how association money is being spent. When tens of thousands of pounds have been raised, for instance, for the purchase of a building freehold, the discussion can become heated. While it is understandable for association committee members to feel hurt by criticism of the volunteer work they are doing, they still have a duty to respond calmly, clearly and helpfully to any and all queries about money and other important association matters.

If there has been a theft of residents' association funds by a committee member or other member, this is obviously a crime and can be reported to the police. However, embarrassment amongst committee members often leads resident groups not to report to the authorities that funds have been embezzled or otherwise misappropriated. If the amount of money taken is relatively small, residents may also feel that reporting the incident to the police would be too distressing for neighbours to make it worthwhile. This is all the more reason for committee members to pursue a policy of transparency and high-quality corporate governance, to minimise the possible abuse of power and misuse of residents' funds.

The FPRA provides some excellent guides on best practice within residents' groups. Contact details are provided in Appendix 1, 'Useful contacts'.

Getting official recognition

A residents' association can begin functioning as soon as it has been set up, even if it only has two members. However, it is only when a residents' association has been officially recognised that it has the full legal rights to be consulted by the landlord on major repairs and other works, and to obtain certain information from the landlord.

There are two ways for a residents' association to gain official recognition. The first is to write to the landlord and request recognition. If the landlord sends written confirmation that he has recognised the residents' association, then no further action need be taken. The landlord is not allowed to withdraw his recognition without providing six months' written notice.

If the landlord refuses to recognise the residents' association, then the group can apply for recognition to the nearest Rent Assessment Panel of the RPTS. The Panels decide, amongst other matters, on whether to grant recognition to residents' associations. (The RPTS calls these groups tenants' associations because, according to English law, leaseholders are tenants.)

The RPTS defines a tenants' association as a group of leaseholders that pay variable service charges – or service charges that vary from year to year, depending on running costs in the building. The RPTS says that the legal rights of an officially-recognised tenants' association include the right to:

- ask the landlord for a summary of service charge costs each year;
- inspect the accounts and receipts;
- propose names of contractors to be considered when major works are to be done;
- request details of the insurance policy for the building; and
- be consulted on the appointment of a managing agent for the building.

In order to apply to a Rent Assessment Panel for official recognition, a residents' association must send:

- a copy of the constitution;
- a list of members and their addresses;
- the name and address of the landlord;
- a description and the address of the building or buildings; and
- copies of any correspondence that is relevant to the application for recognition, including correspondence with the landlord.

When deciding whether to grant official recognition, the Rent Assessment Panel will look at several factors, including the number of members. The RPTS says that the Rent Assessment Panels usually expect at least 60 per cent of qualified residents in a building to belong to the association. The Panels also look at whether the association is run in a manner that is 'fair and democratic', including whether it has proper rules regarding the:

- openness of membership;
- election of a secretary, chairperson and other officers;

- payment of a subscription and the amount payable;

- annual meetings;

- notices of other meetings;

- voting arrangements and quorum (only one vote per flat or house is permitted);

- independence from the landlord.

When a residents' association applies for recognition by sending a letter and relevant enclosures, the Rent Assessment Panel then normally sends a copy of these documents to the landlord. The Panel asks the landlord to explain in writing why he is refusing recognition and the Panel copies these documents to the residents' association. The RPTS says that the Panel cannot accept any documentation that is sent with the words 'without prejudice' or 'in confidence'.

If the Panel grants recognition, it issues the residents' association with a certificate of recognition which is usually valid for four years. The Panel can cancel a certificate at any time if it considers that the residents' association no longer merits recognition. The issue of recognition is normally decided purely by correspondence and there is no charge for the application. More information is provided at the RPTS website at www.rpts.gov.uk.

A residents' association that is refused recognition should not necessarily be discouraged. It is still a real association. It simply lacks the legal right to demand certain consultation with and information from the landlord.

The success factors for residents' associations

Serving as a committee member of a large residents' association can seem a thankless task. There are countless reports of residents contacting committee members late on a Sunday night to ask for help with a leaky tap or to make a complaint about a noisy neighbour that really should be directed at the landlord or managing agent. It can also be difficult to get big projects done, given the fact that committee members are unpaid volunteers with little formal authority. Momentum in a building can disappear when one or more project organisers move out or lose interest. Committee members can maximise the chances of project success and avoid tears by addressing head on some of the unique aspects of the residents' group.

Strong leadership while avoiding dictatorship

Committee members need to show strong leadership skills while avoiding the common occurrence of allowing the head of the association or another committee member to become a virtual dictator in the building. Committee members can tackle the danger of apathy and delay by sending association members informative update notes and keeping them involved in big projects.

One serious complaint is that committee members in some buildings allow members to use the association as a forum for launching personal attacks on neighbours. Committee members need to make clear that the association provides equal representation to all members and that it has no mandate for resolving bilateral disputes amongst neighbours.

Service charge disputes

A common cause for the collapse of residents' associations over the years has been the 'rent strike'. Because leaseholders used to have so little power to force landlords to provide a good service in managing the building, many exasperated leaseholders would simply withhold their service charges. While this may have produced a satisfying feeling of revenge in the short term, this type of rent strike has caused many residents' associations to lose support and fall apart as people move from a building and pay up their past-due service charges on their way out.

Residents in many buildings with rent strikes have indeed wanted to buy their freehold, but the association failed to make clear the binary strategic options of fighting the landlord or else getting rid of the landlord. Residents that get bogged down for years in rent strikes are far less likely to succeed in buying their freehold than those that focus clearly on the end goal of enfranchisement. The most effective residents' associations are those that rally support for forward-moving projects, such as collective enfranchisement, group lease extensions or the right to manage. Those that spend time trying to settle old scores with the landlord often disintegrate after a few years.

Organisational structure in a residents' association

In order for committee members to run residents' associations effectively, they need to recognise the dramatically different nature of the association as compared to the landlord. This becomes particularly important when an association is moving ahead with a big project such as buying the freehold.

The residents' association is, by nature, an organisation with a flat hierarchy. While committee members are elected, they have little real authority with which to get things done. They cannot sack one another, for instance, if a job is not done properly or on time, in the manner that one might expect in the more accountable environment of a commercial enterprise. In order to move forward with important projects, committee members first need to build a sense of trust, shared purpose and commitment amongst members. It is also difficult for a residents' association to initiate and complete big projects since each committee member does this work on a part-time, unpaid basis, while understandably dedicating most of his time and focus to the day job and family.

In stark contrast to this is the vertical hierarchical structure of the landlord, whether an individual or a large corporate entity. One of the most important business-critical roles of the landlord is to protect and maximise the value of his property assets. This is normally the full-time paid occupation of the landlord. When the landlord is a large company, there is usually a clearly-defined line of command within the organisation, staffed by full-time paid employees.

Committees need to recognise the special challenges that result from the different structures of the residents' association and the landlord. Even in cases where the landlord is responsive to residents' needs and provides a good service in the building, the residents' association suffers from a David-and-Goliath mismatch in terms of power and clout. Because of this, residents' associations need to be especially focused about what they are trying to achieve. The committee needs to help association members select goals carefully and to avoid trying to fight too many battles at one time. In this way, the committee can build strong momentum and minimise the organisational disadvantage that virtually every residents' association suffers vis-à-vis the landlord.

The residents' association versus the resident management company

Residents need to avoid confusion about the status and responsibilities of a residents' association as compared to an RMC. As we saw in chapter 3, 'Buying the freehold', the RMC is the limited company set up by leaseholders to act initially as nominee purchaser, for the purpose of buying the freehold of the building. This is different from the RTM, or right to manage, company we examined in chapter 6, 'The right to manage', which is created by leaseholders in order to take over management of the building. The shareholders of the RMC, the enfranchising residents, own the company and appoint directors to run it. The directors are obliged by law to run the RMC in a manner that is fully compliant with the Companies Act. As is the case with all limited companies in England and Wales, an RMC must have at least one director and a company secretary, and these cannot be the same person.

The directors of the RMC must ensure that the company files all necessary documentation with Companies House, the government body that registers all companies and maintains their public files. Failure to do so can result in the company being 'struck off' at Companies House, the legal equivalent of a company being declared dead. Having the company brought back to life, or 'restored', can cost more than £1,000 and require months of work in liaising with the relevant government bodies.

The legal structure of a residents' association is far looser and the legal obligations of committee members vaguely-defined. It is not accurate to assume that members of the residents' association literally own the association, as is the case with shareholders of an RMC. Confusion can occur when leaseholders set up a residents' association and later establish an RMC, and the people in charge fail to distinguish properly between the two separate organisations and their different mandates.

Organising and completing the project of buying a freehold can take years in a large building, especially if the landlord is resisting the purchase, so residents must be prepared for the possibility that a residents' association and an RMC will co-exist side by side for a few years. Some people might belong to the residents' association but not be shareholders of the RMC, so committee members and directors need to take care to distribute the correct information to the relevant group. To cut down on costs, the AGM of the association and the RMC can be held on the same day, back-to-back, in the same venue.

Compliance for resident management companies

As we have seen above, good corporate governance and compliance are important for the residents' association, but these are do-or-die issues for the RMC since it must comply with the Companies Act and other regulations related to limited companies. The directors of a limited company in England and Wales have clearly-defined legal obligations and liabilities in the running of the company.

None of this should cause panic for residents that are contemplating setting up an RMC in order to enfranchise. Participants in the enfranchisement need simply to be aware of the legal nature of the limited company, and the legal roles and responsibilities of company directors. Enfranchisement organisers that set up and are possibly involved in the running of an RMC must ensure good corporate governance from the beginning, rather than wait until the freehold purchase has been completed.

Unfortunately, this is easier said than done. According to Anthony Essien, Principal Advisor at the Leasehold Advisory Service, the RMC is the one category of company most often struck off by Companies House. As of January 2005, Companies House reported the existence of 50,113 RMCs in England and Wales, as registered under the Standard Industrial Classification (SIC) code 9800 for 'Residents Property Management Companies'. It is not clear whether all 50,113 are true RMCs or whether other companies have been included in this grouping. What is known is that an average 100 RMCs are struck off at Companies House each year. This usually happens as a result of a failure by the company to file its annual return and/or financial accounts with Companies House.

In establishing good housekeeping, the RMC needs to ensure compliance in company activities such as:

- adopting Memorandum and Articles of Association;
- issuing share certificates to shareholders;
- holding the AGM;
- keeping minutes of the AGM;
- organising and supervising the election of directors;
- holding and keeping minutes of board meetings;
- getting the year-end financial accounts prepared;
- filing the year-end financial accounts with Companies House;
- filing the annual return with Companies House;
- filing updated lists of directors and shareholders with Companies House.

Outsourcing non-strategic functions

It is a common mistake for directors of an RMC to try to do too much of the non-strategic work themselves. Since RMC directors normally do the company work on an unpaid basis, it is essential to develop working procedures that ensure compliance, but also cut down on time and effort.

For this reason, RMCs are strongly advised to outsource activities such as the initial formation of the company and the ongoing work of the company secretary. Companies such as Jordans Limited specialise in this type of company formation and company secretarial work. By spending a few hundred pounds each year, the RMC ensures that all necessary documents are filed on time with Companies House and that other necessary paperwork is done in a cost-effective manner. This includes the printing of company shares, which can be time-consuming in a block of flats where people come and go and flats are sold each year. RMCs are also advised to outsource the preparation of the year-end financial accounts to a qualified accountancy firm. Asking a resident in the building to do this work on an unpaid basis represents a false economy if the accounts are prepared incorrectly or filing deadlines at Companies House are missed.

RMC directors must not outsource the top-level responsibility of ensuring compliance and probity in the running of the company. They should also not outsource the strategic function of identifying with shareholders which big projects to pursue and keeping them informed of important developments.

Building competence on the board of directors

It can be challenging for a residents' group to identify qualified members that are willing to volunteer their time to serve as directors of an RMC. While it is useful to have RMC directors that already have previous experience as company directors, it is not absolutely necessary. Those without experience can easily get the required training. Regardless of directors' past experience, it is essential that they understand how a limited company works, including the fact that the company is owned by the shareholders, and that the shareholders both elect the directors to run the company and can remove the directors. The board of directors is accountable to the shareholders, but not for the operational decision-making and day-to-day running of the company. The directors are responsible for this.

It is best practice for limited companies, including RMCs, to get directors' insurance and for the company to pay for this. This is insurance coverage against any possible law suit against a company director in his capacity as director. Having such directors' insurance can help encourage highly-qualified individuals to agree to serve on the board.

Some of the most effective RMC boards of directors are those that achieve diversity across age, gender and cultural lines, and that bring to the company different types of experience. While it is useful to have people on the RMC board with corporate, legal and/or accounting experience, it is essential to have directors with integrity and a commitment to serve residents in the building. Strong organisational and communications skills also distinguish the most successful RMCs from those that have trouble building consensus and getting things done.

CHAPTER 10
From leasehold to rental

While England and Wales have an estimated 1.5 million leasehold flats according to government statistics, or some four million according to industry experts, there is also a significant number of flats rented directly from the landlord or freeholder. Indeed, prior to 1914, about 90 per cent of all housing in the United Kingdom was rented. Then a big change took place. Between the First and the Second World Wars, the government placed tight restrictions on landlords through a series of Rent Acts that limited the ability of landlords to increase rent and evict tenants. These laws had the unintended effect of drying up the rental apartment market in urban centres such as London, where many landlords concluded it was uneconomical to rent out their properties. Beginning in the 1950s an increasing number of freeholders opted to sell long leases to their flats, with a long lease defined as having more than 21 years at the start. Most long leases granted were for 99 or 125 years, although many were granted in central London for shorter terms. By 1991, only seven per cent of Britons were renting their homes.

So what happens when the term of a long lease expires? Special regulations have been created to protect the right of the long leaseholder once his lease runs out. In most cases, the resident will be able to continue living in the flat, but there will no longer be a lease. Instead, the resident will become a renting tenant. The rights and obligations of the resident and the landlord will now be defined in a new document, the tenancy agreement. While the resident will no longer own any equity or property once the lease expires, the law protects his right to remain in the flat and rent it from the landlord for a reasonable amount of money. This chapter examines the different types of rental tenancies and reviews the process by which a leasehold flat can be transformed into a rental property when the lease expires.

Different types of rental tenancy

If a visitor walks into a large mansion block in central London, he is likely to encounter many residents that are leaseholders. However, a number of people in the block might be renting their flats directly from the landlord. If the building is owned privately, whether by a person, company or other entity, these renters will usually have one of the following three types of tenancy:

1. a regulated tenancy (also called protected tenancy);

2. an assured tenancy (also called full assured tenancy or ordinary assured tenancy); or

3. an assured shorthold tenancy.

The type of rental tenancy a resident will have depends mainly on when the tenancy was created. The three main types of rental tenancy are described below.

Regulated tenancy

Regulated tenancies are the oldest of the three main categories of modern rental tenancies. Regulated tenants in England and Wales enjoy the highest level of protection against large increases in rent and eviction. Many regulated tenants, who are also called 'sitting tenants', 'protected tenants' or 'Rent Act tenants', are senior citizens. This is because this type of tenancy dates back to the Rent Act 1977 and normally only covers tenancy agreements that were reached before January 1989. A regulated tenant has long-term security of tenure and the landlord is only permitted to raise the rent by a limited amount in any given year. The rent that is paid by regulated tenants is normally significantly lower than the market rate and is established by a Rent Officer. The Rent Officer, whose role will be discussed below, usually registers the rent for a period of two years. This sets a maximum level beyond which the landlord cannot charge. Advisors who assist private property investors often recommend that they avoid buying buildings with large numbers of regulated tenancies. This is because the landlords of these buildings have more restricted ability to raise rents.

Assured tenancy

By the 1980s, many members of the public and people in government, business and other sectors recognised that the restrictions that had been previously placed on landlords were hurting the ability of the property sector to develop. This was, in turn, limiting the number of rental flats available to consumers. With the Housing Act 1988 important steps were taken to enable landlords to charge rent at a market rate. The 1988 Act created the assured tenancy, which covered both ordinary assured tenancies and assured shorthold tenancies. In this chapter, to help identify and highlight the differences, we will refer to assured tenancies and shorthold tenancies.

Assured tenancies and shorthold tenancies both made it possible for the landlord to charge a market rent, but each type provided the renter with a different level of security of tenure. The person renting a flat on an assured tenancy has the right to remain in the property on an ongoing basis, unless the landlord can prove to a court that he has grounds for possession of the flat. With an assured tenancy, the landlord does not have an automatic right to repossess the flat when the tenancy comes to an end. When a long leaseholder's lease expires and the resident stays on in the same flat, this is normally done by becoming an assured tenant. This is explained below.

Shorthold tenancy

The shorthold tenancy provides the renter with less security of tenure than the assured tenancy. If a landlord is renting out a flat on a shorthold tenancy, he has the right to regain possession of the property six months after the beginning of the tenancy, as long as the landlord gives the resident two months' notice. Assured and shorthold tenancies were created by the Housing Act 1988, but there was an important change in legislation eight years later. According to the Housing Act 1996, any tenancy created on or after 28 February 1997 is automatically a shorthold tenancy, unless special steps are taken to set up an assured tenancy. Previously, the tenant got the greater security by default. Any tenancy created before 28 February 1997 had automatically been an assured tenancy, unless a special procedure was followed to set up a shorthold tenancy.

If one arrives in London from another part of the United Kingdom or from overseas in search of a rental flat, one is most likely to rent under a shorthold tenancy. This is the most common type of tenancy in the private residential sector in England and Wales.

Assured periodic tenancy

A shorthold tenancy is for a fixed term, such as six or 12 months. At the end of the term, if no action is taken by the landlord or resident, the tenancy automatically becomes what is called an 'assured periodic tenancy'. This is also known as a 'statutory periodic tenancy'. This means that the tenancy will automatically run on from one rent period to the next, on the same rent and the same terms as the preceding fixed-term shorthold tenancy. The tenancy, which no longer has a fixed term, will continue unless it is ended by the landlord or the resident, or is replaced by a different tenancy.

Similarly, when an assured tenancy ends, if no action is taken by the landlord or the resident, then the assured tenancy will run on with the same rent and terms as before and it will now be called a 'statutory periodic tenancy'. Alternatively, the landlord and tenant can agree a replacement fixed-term assured tenancy, or a replacement assured tenancy on a periodic basis, called a 'contractual periodic tenancy'.

The following cannot be assured or shorthold tenancies:

*   A tenancy that started before 15 January 1989.

*   A tenancy for which the rent is more than £25,000 per year.

*   A tenancy that is rent-free or for which the rent is £1,000 or less in Greater London, or £250 or less per year elsewhere in England and Wales.

*   A business tenancy.

*   A tenancy of a property rented with more than two acres of agricultural land.

- A tenancy granted to a student by an educational body.

- A holiday let.

- A letting by a resident landlord.

- A tenancy where the property is owned by the Crown.

- A tenancy where the landlord is a local authority or certain housing associations.

The following can be assured tenancies, but not shorthold tenancies:

- A tenancy replacing an earlier assured tenancy with the same tenant.

- An assured tenancy that was passed on to a tenant on the death of the previous regulated tenant, regarding a pre-1989 tenancy agreement.

- An assured tenancy following a secure tenancy after a property has been transferred to a private landlord from a public sector landlord.

- An assured tenancy resulting from the expiry of a long leasehold tenancy.

Tenancies for buy-to-let properties

A landlord that lets a flat on an assured or shorthold tenancy may be a large company that is the freeholder of the building or an individual who is the leaseholder of the flat. In the latter case, the leaseholder sublets his unit and thus becomes the immediate landlord of the sub-lessee. Most buy-to-let property investors now rent out their flats on shorthold tenancies, since these enable the leaseholder to charge the market rent and to regain possession of the flat later on.

Ending a tenancy

For tenancies that started on or after 28 February 1997, landlords have a right to regain possession of the rented property without giving any grounds for repossession, as long as notice is provided at least six months after the start of the original tenancy and as long as at least two months' notice is given. If a shorthold tenant receives notice that the landlord wants possession, but the tenant refuses to leave, the landlord can apply to a court to start possession proceedings. Landlords are not allowed to evict tenants themselves. If the court approves the possession, then the court will arrange for bailiffs to evict the tenant.

It is more difficult for a landlord to regain possession from an assured tenant, since this tenancy provides a higher level of security of tenure. If an assured tenant does not wish to leave a flat or house, the landlord can seek a possession order from the court on one or more grounds, such as the following:

- The property is subject to a mortgage and the lender wants to sell it.

- The tenant owes at least two months' rent.

- The tenant has been persistently late in paying his rent.

- The tenant has broken one or more terms of the tenancy agreement.

- The tenant has caused a nuisance or annoyance to someone living in the locality.

- The landlord was persuaded to grant the tenancy on the basis of a false statement.

Limits on rent increases

Although regulated tenants enjoy the highest level of protection against large rent increases in private property, assured and shorthold tenants are also protected by law against unreasonable rent hikes. Landlords are not allowed to raise rent within a fixed-term tenancy, unless the tenant agrees. If it is a periodic tenancy, according to the Housing Act 1988, the landlord must notify the tenant in writing using a special form called 'Landlord's Notice Proposing A New Rent Under An Assured Periodic Tenancy Or Agricultural Occupancy'. The landlord must give the tenant at least one month's notice of the proposed rent increase. If the tenant agrees to the new rent amount, then this new rent takes effect.

If an assured or shorthold tenant believes the rent or rent increase is unreasonable, he has the right to challenge the amount. If a person is renting a flat or house under a shorthold tenancy, he must submit the challenge within the first six months of the tenancy. To challenge the reasonableness of rent or a rent increase, the tenant must apply to a Rent Assessment Committee.

The Rent Assessment Committee

As we have seen, the regional Rent Assessment Panels in England and Wales are part of the Residential Property Tribunal Service (RPTS). Each Rent Assessment Panel – the London Panel has 90 members – appoints Rent Assessment Committees to hear and decide on each case. Each Committee normally comprises three members, a lawyer, a valuer and a layperson. Addresses of the Rent Assessment Panels are contained in Appendix 1, 'Useful contacts'.

The Rent Assessment Committee will take into account the written information that has been submitted by each party, including the tenancy agreement and information about rents being charged for comparable properties in the same area. The Committee will decide what is the rent that the landlord could reasonably expect for the property if it were let on the open market under a new tenancy. The Rent Assessment Committee can decide on a rent that is lower, higher or the same as that being requested by the landlord. Once the Committee has fixed the rent, the landlord cannot charge more than this for the following year.

According to the Housing Act 1996, tenants may only apply to the Rent Assessment Committee within six months of the beginning of the original tenancy. A shorthold tenant is not allowed to refer the rent a second time to the Committee.

When assured, shorthold or regulated tenants challenge the reasonableness of the rent they are being charged, they usually represent themselves before the Rent Assessment Committee. They can also be represented by a family member, friend or colleague. Although they have the right to be represented by a solicitor or other advisor, it is unusual for residents to go to this expense. Most landlords, on the other hand, are represented by a solicitor or estate agent.

The Rent Officer

When Rent Officers work with residents in the private property sector, they are often working with regulated tenants. The regulated tenant enjoys strong protection against high rent increases because a maximum allowable rent for these flats is registered, and thus fixed, by a Rent Officer. Rent Officers work for The Rent Service, which is an executive agency of the Department for Work and Pensions. The Rent Service, which was created in October 1999, says that it aims to be England's leading provider of impartial, professional rental valuation services. The agency's main areas of focus are to:

- provide rental valuations for Housing Benefit purposes, to identify whether Housing Benefit claimants are being overcharged rent by landlords;

- make 'fair rent' determinations;

- advise local authorities on the impact on rent of housing renovation grant applications by landlords; and

- carry out rental valuations for other customers in the public and private sectors.

Contact information for The Rent Service is provided in Appendix 1, 'Useful contacts'.

The registered rent for a flat is public domain information and is available for inspection by members of the public at the RPTS's main office. When leaseholders in a block of flats are considering whether to buy the freehold, they are well-advised to get all relevant information, including the registered rents and other terms, for any regulated tenants in the building.

If a landlord or a regulated tenant wishes to challenge the rent determination of a Rent Officer, he may do so by applying to a Rent Assessment Committee at the RPTS.

When a lease expires

When a long lease expires, the leaseholder has the right in most cases to stay on in the flat and to do so under an assured periodic tenancy. This right is laid out in Schedule 10 of the Local Government and Housing Act 1989, which we will call 'Schedule 10'. (Previously, this right was covered under Part I of the Landlord and Tenant Act 1954.)

A leaseholder wishing to secure an assured periodic tenancy in a flat after the lease has run out must be using the unit as his principal home at the time of the lease expiry.

Schedule 10 does not apply to all leasehold properties. Properties belonging to the Crown, to a local authority and to certain housing associations, for instance, are excluded. If the leaseholder has gained a lease extension under the Leasehold Reform, Housing and Urban Development Act 1993, then he is not entitled to continued tenancy after the extended lease expires. However, if the owner got a lease extension to a house under the Leasehold Reform Act 1967, then Schedule 10 does apply and the resident does have the right to continued tenancy.

When a long lease expires, it is the landlord rather than the leaseholder who is required to complete and send certain documentation. If the landlord agrees to the resident's wish for continued tenancy, then he must send to the resident a form that is prescribed by law and that is called 'Form No. 1: Landlord's Notice Terminating A Long Residential Tenancy And Proposing An Assured Monthly Periodic Tenancy'. The landlord must normally send this form no sooner than 12 months and no later than six months before the date on which the lease will expire. Once the tenant receives the form, he can agree the terms of the assured periodic tenancy with the landlord. Written notice of acceptance should be sent to the landlord within two months of receipt of the offer. If an assured periodic tenancy is agreed, then the tenant is protected against eviction under the Housing Act 1988.

If the resident disagrees with the proposed terms, then he must write to the landlord and present a counter-offer of terms. This must be done by sending a form called 'Form No. 4: Tenant's Notice Proposing Different Rent Or Terms For An Assured Periodic Tenancy'. If Form No. 4 is used, it must be sent to the landlord within two months of receiving the landlord's offer. If the tenant and landlord do not agree on the terms of the assured periodic tenancy, then the landlord can apply to a Rent Assessment Committee, which will decide on the terms. The landlord does this by sending to the Rent Assessment Committee 'Form No. 5: Landlord's Application Referring A Tenant's Notice Proposing Different Rent Or Terms For An Assured Periodic Tenancy, To A Rent Assessment Committee'. The landlord must do this within two months of receiving the tenant's counter-offer of terms. If he fails to do so within the two months, then the terms proposed by the tenant in Form No. 4 take effect at the end of the lease.

If the landlord wishes to gain possession of the flat, he sends to the tenant 'Form No. 2: Landlord's Notice Terminating A Long Residential Tenancy And Proposing To Apply To Court For Possession'. There are limited grounds on which a landlord can refuse to provide an assured periodic tenancy to a resident whose long lease has expired. The possible grounds include that:

- the landlord intends to demolish or reconstruct the building;
- suitable alternative accommodation has been found for the tenant;
- the tenant owes rent or has been consistently late in paying rent;
- one or more obligations under the lease have been broken; and
- the tenant has caused a nuisance or annoyance to people in the local area.

If the landlord wishes for the tenant to leave, then he must apply to the County court for a possession order. The tenant cannot be made to leave unless the court orders possession for the landlord.

It is important to note that fewer and fewer leaseholders these days allow the terms of their leases to get so low as to have to contemplate losing all equity in the property and becoming a renting tenant. Indeed, the leading valuers and estate agents in central London say that they each get only a handful of cases each year where leaseholders have allowed the lease to get down to the single-digit level. In a growing number of cases, leaseholders resolve the problem of the short lease either by getting a 90-year lease extension or by teaming up with their fellow residents in order to buy the freehold of the building.

CHAPTER 11

Restrictions that won't go away

This book has described several ways in which leaseholders have gained new rights in recent years regarding their leasehold properties. However, several restrictions remain in place that prevent leaseholders' full control over these assets. This includes leasehold property that falls within categories that are exempt from enfranchisement legislation. This chapter describes some of the main exempt areas.

Estate management schemes

Estate management schemes are those that provide the landlord with certain management control over residential properties, including after leaseholders have bought the freehold. The aim in creating these schemes was to ensure that the appearance of a residential area as a whole, such as a row of houses, was maintained to the same quality even after leaseholders bought the freehold. In addition to applying to buildings comprising leasehold property, estate management schemes can apply to communal gardens and other common outdoor grounds.

The legislation covering estate management schemes dates back to the 1960s. The Leasehold Reform Act 1967 gave landlords of leasehold houses the right to apply for estate management schemes, which gave them certain management rights for the general benefit of the neighbourhood.

Landlords secured the right to apply for estate management schemes regarding leasehold flats under the Leasehold Reform, Housing and Urban Development Act 1993. The 1993 Act transferred responsibility for decisions about estate management schemes from the courts to the Leasehold Valuation Tribunal (LVT).

Although estate management schemes leave the landlord with certain management control over the property, leaseholders have the right to challenge the relevant management fees, if they believe these are unreasonable, by applying to the LVT. Leaseholders can also apply to the LVT to have an estate management scheme 'varied' or changed. Finally, estate management schemes are required to contain one or more clauses that allow for the scheme to be changed or terminated. Many schemes will allow for leaseholders to apply to the LVT for a scheme to be ended, while some older estate management schemes require an application to the High Court. Leaseholders need to check on the specific provisions in the scheme.

If an individual leaseholder or a group of residents wishes to apply to the LVT to challenge the reasonableness of management fees charged under an estate management scheme, or if they wish to have the scheme changed or ended, they must include the following information in their application:

• The names and addresses of the applicant(s) and the landlord or holder of the estate management scheme.

• The address of the premises to which the scheme applies.

• A copy of the estate management scheme.

• A statement that the applicant is a person or a body authorised to represent the applicant(s) according to Sections 71(3) or 71(5) of the Leasehold Reform, Housing and Urban Development Act 1993.

• A statement that the applicant believes the information provided in the application to be true.

If leaseholders want to enfranchise a block of flats or house that is subject to an estate management scheme, usually they may do so, but they will still be subject to paying an annual charge for the upkeep of the area after the freehold acquisition. If an application has been made for the creation of an estate management scheme, then enfranchising leaseholders must wait for this to be concluded before they can proceed with their enfranchisement.

Crown property

One of the important categories of residential property that is exempt from enfranchisement legislation is Crown property. The land and buildings owned by Queen Elizabeth in her capacity as monarch, known as the Crown Estate, represent one of the largest and most valuable property portfolios in the UK. Much of the Sovereign's landholdings date back to 1066, the time of the Norman Conquest. The Crown Estate is worth about £1.6 billion and includes retail buildings valued at £800 million and residential property worth some £520 million. There are more than 2,600 residential buildings, which include about 10,000 letting agreements, within the Crown Estate throughout the country.

The Crown Estate says that it pays all of its net revenue each year, about £170 million, to the British Treasury. In the last year, the value of Crown Estate property has increased by 146 per cent, with revenue shooting up by 130 per cent. Crown property accounts for large swathes of some of London's most prestigious real estate, including Regent's Street, parts of Kensington, Victoria, St James's, Millbank and the West End. Kensington Palace Gardens, an exclusive road adjacent to Kensington Palace, is home to many embassies and luxury homes.

When legislation was passed to give leaseholders of houses and flats the right to enfranchise, Crown property was exempted. However, the Crown has taken a somewhat flexible approach towards enfranchisement. When the Leasehold Reform, Housing and Urban Development Act 1993 was passed, the Crown made an important statement through a government minister at the time that it would, where possible, follow the spirit of the enfranchisement law and allow leaseholders collectively to buy their freehold if they would otherwise have qualified.

The Crown Estate says it always considers the sale of building freeholds or 90-year lease extensions to leaseholders that would have qualified for these legal rights in non-Crown properties. While the Crown dates back further than other big landlords in the United Kingdom, the Crown says it has effectively stayed ahead of enfranchisement legislation in this area. Although it does not release numbers of freeholds sold, property experts say that the Crown Estate has quietly sold off dozens of its houses and blocks of flats in London to leaseholders.

Land and buildings owned by the Crown Estate are held in a trustee capacity and the Crown says that it places strong emphasis on its stewardship responsibilities. For this reason, the Crown Estate refuses to sell to leaseholders those properties that have special historic significance, such as the 460 houses and blocks of flats in and around Regent's Park in London. The Crown Estate owns more than 1,000 listed buildings across the United Kingdom, a third of which are Grade I. Of all the listed buildings in the country, just three per cent are Grade I.

Although the Crown Estate has been willing, in many instances, to agree a negotiated freehold sale with leaseholders, the procedure appears recently to have been tightened and formalised. Several freehold sales have been negotiated since the 1990s on a fairly informal basis, but estate agents representing the Crown Estate recently said that leaseholders wanting to buy their freehold must follow the enfranchisement procedure, including serving a formal enfranchisement notice.

National Trust property

Residential property that is built on certain land held by the National Trust or charitable housing trusts is also exempt from enfranchisement legislation. The National Trust owns more than 248,000 hectares (612,000 acres) of land in England, Wales and Northern Ireland, over 200 buildings and gardens, and nearly 600 miles of coastline. It is a registered charity that holds its land and other property in perpetuity. The National Trust has special statutory powers that enable it to declare its property 'inalienable', meaning the property cannot be sold, mortgaged or compulsorily purchased against the wishes of the trust.

CONCLUSION

Leaseholders in England and Wales have had good reason to complain over the years. They have enjoyed far more limited rights of ownership and control than a vast majority of equivalent homeowners in other industrialised nations. Complex land law, much of it dating back to the feudal age, has provided enormous protection for landlords, often to the detriment of leasehold homeowners.

The limited manner in which leaseholders actually own their homes has had several negative knock-on effects on residential property, the quality of neighbourhoods and the economy at large. While resident owners of apartment buildings in New York or Paris are able to make rapid decisions on collectively investing money to improve and upgrade their buildings, such improvements can take decades in London, since many absentee corporate landlords see little financial incentive in pushing ahead with such works.

Flat owners in England and Wales continue to suffer from an outdated leasehold system in which they bear the full cost and risk of managing their block of flats, while seeing control over the building remain in the hands of the landlord. As a result, the leaseholders of mansion blocks and other large purpose-built blocks of flats are often stymied in their efforts to spend their money on upgrading their building with cable or satellite television, a building-wide broadband system or new CCTV security cameras. This structural obstacle to building improvements discourages consumer spending and the type of development that enhances quality of life in neighbourhoods.

The good news is that legislation created since 1993 has begun to equip leaseholders with some basic rights needed in order to enjoy fuller ownership and control of their homes. These laws have been a long time coming and have represented efforts by governments led by both the Conservative and the Labour Parties to reform the leasehold system. The task has not been completed, however, since the laws affecting leaseholders remain too complex, unwieldy and skewed in favour of landlords' rights.

The change in law, a growing allure associated with apartment living and the internationalisation of London's residential property market have all fuelled the emergence of a strong consumer trend amongst leaseholders. Flat owners have grown increasingly impatient with outdated legislation that creates obstacles to their collectively owning and controlling buildings the cost of which they already cover. This new homeowner mindset is likely to result in a growing number of enfranchisements and to improvements in many of the multiple-resident buildings that have been neglected for decades.

This book has covered many aspects of the leasehold system, from the creation of a residents' association to the running of a resident management company (RMC). We have examined leaseholders' rights to get a 90-year lease extension and to the newly-won ability for residents to get the right to manage their building without proving fault on the part of the landlords. Several chapters have addressed the ways in which leaseholders can acquire their building, including freehold purchase by negotiation, right of first refusal and enfranchisement.

Equipped with these new rights, leaseholders in England and Wales can now begin to grow up as true homeowners. Flat owners need to dedicate increasing focus on learning about their rights as leaseholders and about changes in residential property legislation. They also must remember that with these new rights come responsibilities. A main challenge in the future will be the creation of an effective set of standards and procedures for residents that own the freehold of their building, including those that serve as directors of an RMC. The directors of many RMC companies are presently struggling to come to grips with the legal responsibilities of company directors and pressing issues regarding financial transparency and corporate governance. The ability of these companies to serve their shareholders and other stakeholders effectively will determine whether this new class of resident landlord represents a real improvement on the outdated freeholder system.

Glossary

absent landlord	A landlord the whereabouts of whom are not known to leaseholders of the property.
appurtenant property	A garage, outhouse, garden, yard, courtyard or other property outside the building, as referred to in enfranchisement notices.
assured tenancy	A tenancy that has security of tenure and other rights under Part I of the Housing Act 1988.
collective enfranchisement	The process by which leaseholders collectively compel the landlord to sell them the freehold of their building, at a fair market price in a statutory timeframe.
common parts	The parts of the building used by all residents, such as the front entrance and lobby, common staircase and common hallways.
commonhold	A type of property ownership that took effect in 2004 that allows freehold ownership of individual flats, houses and non-residential units within a building or estate. Possession by commonhold, which is an alternative to the leasehold system, is not limited by time as with a lease.
covenant	A legally-binding promise, as referred to in leases.
demised	The grant of a leasehold interest, as referred to in leases.
demised premises	The flat or house that is the subject of the lease.

freeholder	The holder of the freehold interest of a property, usually the landlord.
head leaseholder	The owner of a superior lease to that held by ordinary leaseholders, but which is not the freehold. This is also known as the party that holds an intermediate interest in a property.
housing association	An organisation, body of trustees or a company that provides or manages housing and that does not operate for a profit. A registered housing association means an association that is registered with the Housing Corporation.
intermediate interest	A middle-level ownership title in a property which is above the level of ordinary leaseholders and below the freeholder. This is also referred to as a head lease.
landlord	The immediate superior property owner above the leaseholders, from whom the leaseholders can seek a lease extension. The landlord is usually the freeholder.
lessee	The tenant or leaseholder.
lessor	The landlord (usually the freeholder).
marriage value	The additional value created in a flat or house by 'marrying' or combining the freehold and leasehold interests. The two interests are combined when leaseholders buy the freehold of the building or, on an individual basis, a leaseholder secures a lease extension for his flat of 90 years or more.
nominee purchaser	The person, company or other entity that buys the freehold of a building in an enfranchisement, on behalf of participating leaseholders.
protected and statutory tenancies	Tenancies that have security of tenure and rent regulation under the Rent Act 1977. Where a protected tenancy comes to an end by a notice to quit, the tenant becomes a statutory tenant provided that he is residing in the premises.
public sector landlord	A landlord such as a local authority, new town corporation or others defined in the Housing Act 1985, Section 1972.

resident landlord	A freeholder or a member of his family who occupies as his only or principal home a flat in a building that is not a purpose-built block.
resident management company	A company owned by residents who in turn collectively own their building or intend to buy the building. Also known as an RMC company.
reversion	The interest in a flat or house that will return to the landlord (freeholder) at the end of the term of the lease.
reversioner	The freeholder or landlord.
right to manage company	A company set up and owned by residents that has the right to manage the building. Also known as an RTM company.
secure tenancy	A tenancy or licence that carries security of tenure, the right-to-buy and other legal rights under the Housing Act 1985. Many secure tenants are tenants of a local authority. Registered housing associations were able to create secure lets before January 1989. Since January 1989, most new lets by housing associations are on assured tenancies.
tenant	A person or entity that holds a tenancy, including a leasehold, of a flat or house and thus has identified rights to occupy and use the property.
term	The number of years granted by the lease, such as 99 years.
underlease	The leasehold title held by the head leaseholder, below the freehold and above the ordinary leaseholders.
unit	A flat.

APPENDIX 1

Useful contacts

Association of Residential Managing Agents (ARMA)
178 Battersea Park Road
London SW11 4ND
Tel: 020 7978 2607
Fax: 020 7498 6153
Email: info@arma.org.uk
Website: www.arma.org.uk

Companies House
Crown Way
Cardiff CF14 3UZ
Tel: 0870 333 3636
Fax: 029 2038 0517
Email: enquiries@companieshouse.gov.uk
Website: www.companieshouse.gov.uk

Federation of Private Residents' Associations (FPRA)
59 Mile End Road
Colchester CO4 5BU
Tel: 0871 200 3324/01206 855 888
Fax: 01206 851 616
Email: info@fpra.org.uk
Website: www.fpra.org.uk

HM Land Registry
Lincoln's Inn Fields
London WC2A 3PH

Tel: 020 7917 8888
Fax: 020 7955 0110
Website: www.landreg.gov.uk *or* www.landregisteronline.gov.uk

Lands Tribunal

48–49 Chancery Lane
London WC2A 1JR
Tel: 020 7936 7000
Website: www.landstribunal.gov.uk

Leasehold Advisory Service ('LEASE')

70–74 City Road
London EC1Y 2BJ
Tel: 020 7490 9580
Fax: 020 7253 2043
Email: info@lease-advice.org
Website: www.lease-advice.org

Leasehold Valuation Tribunals and Rent Assessment Panels

Website: www.rpts.gov.uk

Eastern

Great Eastern House, Tenison Road
Cambridge CB1 2TR
Tel: 0845 100 2616
Fax: 01223 505 116
Email: eastern.rap@odpm.gsi.gov.uk

London

10 Alfred Place
London WC1E 7LR
Tel: 020 7446 7700
Fax: 020 7637 1250
Email: london.rap@odpm.gsi.gov.uk

Midlands

2nd Floor, East Wing, Ladywood House
45–46 Stephenson Street
Birmingham B2 4DH
Tel: 0845 100 2615
Fax: 0121 643 7605
Email: midland.rap@odpm.gsi.gov.uk

Northern

20th Floor, Sunley Tower
Piccadilly Plaza
Manchester M1 4BE
Tel: 0845 100 2614
Fax: 0161 237 3656
Email: northern.rap@odpm.gsi.gov.uk

Southern

1st Floor, 1 Market Avenue
Chichester PO19 1JU
Tel: 0845 100 2617
Fax: 01243 779 389
Email: southern.rap@odpm.gsi.gov.uk

Office of the Deputy Prime Minister

Leasehold Reform Division
Zone 2/J6
Eland House
Bressenden Place
London SW1E 5DU
Tel: 020 7944 4400
Fax: 020 7944 3519
Website: www.odpm.gov.uk

The Rent Service

Head Office
5 Welbeck Street
London W1G 9YQ
Tel: 020 7023 6000
Website: www.therentservice.gov.uk

Residential Property Tribunal Service
(see also Leasehold Valuation Tribunals)

10 Alfred Place
London WC1E 7LR
Tel: 020 7446 7700
Fax: 020 7637 1250
Email: london.rap@odpm.gsi.gov.uk
Website: www.rpts.gov.uk

Royal Institution of Chartered Surveyors
Surveyor Court
Westwood Way
Coventry CV4 8JE
Tel: 0870 333 1600
Fax: 020 7334 3811
Email: contactrics@rics.org
Website: www.rics.org

The Stationery Office
PO Box 29
Norwich NR3 1GN
Tel: 0870 600 5522
Fax: 0870 600 5533
Email: customer.services@tso.co.uk
Website: www.tso.co.uk

Welsh Assembly Government
Housing Directorate
Cathays Park
Cardiff CF10 3NQ
Tel: 029 2082 5111
Fax: 029 2082 6989
Email: housingintranet@wales.gsi.gov.uk
Website: www.wales.gsi.gov.uk

APPENDIX 2

Case studies

Case study A: Negotiated acquisition of freehold

Background information

In July 2001, Heather Darnell and her fiancé bought a flat in a six-storey Edwardian building in London's Notting Hill Gate. When they moved in, leases for the six flats in the building had 75 years left and leaseholders had begun the process of buying the freehold. Residents had decided to pursue this initiative in order to avoid paying the landlord for expensive lease extensions and because they wanted to gain management control over the building. One of the leaseholders' main goals was to get rid of a managing agent that had been hired years earlier by the landlord and who was not providing a cost-effective, customer-friendly service for leaseholders.

What happened

With all six leaseholders in the building participating, preparation work for buying the freehold had started in 2000. They hired a solicitor and also had a surveyor carry out a valuation of the freehold. In 2001, the leaseholders served an enfranchisement notice on the landlord in which they formally advised that they were going to buy the freehold and offered £20,000. The landlord then served a counter-notice on the leaseholders in which he demanded £25,000 for the freehold.

When the leaseholders received the counter-notice, they had to decide whether to fight for a price lower than £25,000 by applying to the Leasehold Valuation Tribunal (LVT) or whether to agree with the landlord on a negotiated acquisition. Going to the LVT would delay the freehold purchase by several months and the leaseholders would be likely to incur additional professional advisors' costs. Although leaseholders are allowed to represent themselves at LVT hearings, it is usual practice for them to hire a solicitor and/or surveyor to represent them and leaseholders have to pay for this. After weeks of discussion, the residents decided to agree with the landlord's counter-offer price and not to go to the LVT. 'The residents decided it was worth it to save the time, trouble and costs of going to the Tribunal,' Heather Darnell said.

In January 2002, the leaseholders completed the purchase of the freehold. They paid just over £1,000 in legal fees, or £175 per flat. As soon as the freehold purchase had been completed, the residents began to manage the building themselves. Darnell said that they decided not to hire another managing agent, since the building was relatively small, leaseholders were proactive and several had commercial, legal or accounting skills that helped in running the building efficiently.

The benefits of freehold purchase

Darnell said that the project of buying the freehold was considered a success by the leaseholders. 'A main benefit was that we got control of our own destiny,' she said. There was an immediate financial benefit, since the main running costs of managing the building were cut in half. The cost of insuring the building each year was slashed to £1,000 from an earlier £3,000, and the leaseholders were able to eliminate an annual £700 management fee that had previously been paid to the managing agent.

Another benefit that leaseholders enjoyed after buying the freehold was seeing the value of the flats in the building shoot up. Flats there which had been valued in 2001 at about £250,000 had risen by 2004 to about £350,000. The price increase was partly due to a general growth in residential property values in the Notting Hill Gate area, but part of the price rise also apparently resulted from the fact that these flats were now 'share of freehold' flats with longer leases.

The problems to avoid

Darnell advises leaseholders to be clear about their own risk profile when they embark on a project to buy their freehold. 'It's important to know whether the residents are willing to fight hard by going to the LVT or whether they will prefer to pay a higher price for the freehold by agreeing to a negotiated settlement,' she said. Darnell said that the DIY approach to building management was working well because she and her neighbours represented an unusually proactive group and several had valuable, relevant skills. Darnell, for instance, runs a business, Back Office Support Systems Limited, that advises small companies on how to set up streamlined financial and administrative processes that save entrepreneurs time, money and effort. Darnell said that leaseholders needed to address frankly and openly any unequal division of labour that can result if one or more leaseholders fail to take an active part in managing the building. 'It's important to be clear about which leaseholders will do which parts of the management work,' she said. 'If any leaseholder does not participate in managing the building, then he should be charged a management fee.'

The lessons learned

Darnell said that the self-management approach that was working well for her and fellow leaseholders would be unsuitable for a building with more than ten flats, because of the complexity of the work involved. She also said that she and her neighbours might hire a managing agent later on, if they needed to get some major repair or renovation work done in the building. 'My advice for leaseholders is to manage the building as much as you can after you buy the freehold, but be sure to get in expert help when you need it,' Darnell said. Her final word of guidance: leaseholders need to be patient when they are in the process of buying the freehold and are waiting for the legal documents to arrive. 'It all takes a while, but it's worth the wait,' she said.

Case study B: Collective enfranchisement

Background information

In 1995, 23-year-old Tara Nealon-Gay moved to the United Kingdom from her home in the United States to join her future husband, who had bought a flat in London. When she arrived, she was shocked by the way residents were treated by the building managing agent. 'I've never seen an agent use the technique of bullying to manage a property the way this agent did,' she said. Over the years she and fellow residents became increasingly exasperated by poor management, shabby building repairs and unreasonably high service charges imposed by the landlord and managing agent. 'The worst aspect was when major works took place, the managing agent would throw in a £4,000 to £5,000 bill to each resident which was due within a 30-day period, as we had no sinking fund,' she said. 'For many of the residents who were self-employed, this was a cashflow nightmare.' Several residents became so angry about the management problems, they refused to pay their service charges. Five years after her arrival in London, Nealon-Gay began to talk with fellow residents about buying the freehold through collective enfranchisement. Initially things got off to a slow start because leaseholders did not know one another, some were absentee and many of the leases had different terms.

What happened

Nealon-Gay said that the situation in her building reached a low point in 1999, when she told the managing agent that, unless the quality of management improved, the leaseholders would simply buy the freehold. 'She (the managing agent) said to me, 'You will never do that.' I could not believe that she said that,' said Nealon-Gay. 'It made me decide to move forward. It seemed incredible that the managing agent could show such arrogance by telling me what I could or could not do.'

There was much organisational work to be done, especially since the building had two different types of leases. Some flats had 72 years left to run, while others had 74 years and one lease had been extended to 189 years. The two sets of leases also had different amounts of ground rent. The project to enfranchise started seriously to move ahead in 2001, with

Nealon-Gay doing the bulk of the research and organising work. 'This was complicated by the fact that me and my husband moved to the Netherlands around that time, so I was managing the project from overseas. Thank goodness for email,' she said.

The residents served an enfranchisement notice on the landlord in August 2002 and offered £80,000 for the freehold. The landlord served a counter-notice in October 2002 demanding four times that amount, with a counter-offer of £330,000. Flats in the building had been valued at £275,000 to £300,000 on average in 2001, and by 2002 had risen some ten to 20 per cent. An LVT hearing was scheduled for 20–21 May 2003.

Four days before the hearing was to begin, the leaseholders reached a negotiated sale price with the landlord of £170,000. Although this was nearly double the original estimate made by the leaseholders' valuer, it had become clear that he had underestimated the rapid rise in market value of flats in the area. By the time the freehold agreement was reached, flats in the building were valued at £396,000 to £466,000.

The benefits of freehold purchase

Nealon-Gay said that enfranchisement required more time, effort and money than originally expected, but the final result of securing total ownership and control of the building by residents was worth it. She said that the resident management company that now owns the freehold and which is collectively owned by the leaseholders has created a sinking fund to smooth out the year-to-year costs of any major works or repairs.

The problems to avoid

Nealon-Gay said that it was essential for leaseholders to gather as much information as possible before starting the formal enfranchisement since it was a complicated process. She said that it was also crucial to instruct solicitors and surveyors who were highly experienced in enfranchisement and to have an overall dedicated project manager to act as the intermediary between all parties. 'They don't just need to be specialists in their specific areas, they also need to be able to communicate in a timely manner with everyone involved in the team,' Nealon-Gay said.

The lessons learned

Nealon-Gay said that she had been shocked by an apparent willingness amongst her neighbours to tolerate abuse at the hands of the managing agent. 'I found it amazing that people accepted this abuse for many years and were bullied into submission. I was brought up to stand up to people and to face them, and not be bullied,' she said. She advised leaseholders to demand their rights, not be bullied by the landlord or managing agent and to gain control of their homes by buying the freehold. 'It has never been an easier time to purchase a freehold. Take advantage of it before the law changes again,' she said.

Speed can be important in an enfranchisement initiative, especially in a rapidly-rising property market. The market values of flats in her building shot up by an estimated 20 per cent during the enfranchisement project and this increased significantly the amount that each participant had to pay for the freehold.

Finally, Nealon-Gay said not to assume that the purchase of one's freehold would eliminate all management headaches. It can be difficult to find a good managing agent which is responsible and addresses possible disputes between residents in a multiple-unit building. When several long-standing owners in her building sold their flats, a new group of sublet residents moved in and began to make a disturbing amount of noise. 'Buying the freehold was definitely worth doing, if only because it solved our problem with short leases,' she said. 'But after you buy the freehold, you have to put in place a good system for enforcing the rules.'

Case study C: The right of first refusal

Background information

Tony Hidden and Michael Fuke had a busy time in 2004 as committee members of the residents' association in their building in Clacton-On-Sea in Essex when the landlord sent a right of first refusal letter offering to sell the freehold to the residents. There was initial confusion when it was discovered that the letter was sent not only to leaseholders in their 19-apartment building, The Towers, but also to a building called The

Turret next door that had 12 apartments. It was unclear precisely what the landlord was offering to sell and, after initial discussions, residents in the two buildings failed to agree on a common way forward. In the meantime, the clock was ticking, since leaseholders must reply within a maximum of two months if they want to buy their building under the right of first refusal process.

What happened

Hidden and Fuke said that the landlord's letter, also called a Section 5 Notice after the relevant piece of legislation, offered £46,500 for what initially appeared to be their building, The Towers. But when the two committee members discovered that the landlord had sent the same letter to the residents next door in The Turret, they realised that they needed to act quickly to clarify matters.

A majority of the leaseholders at The Towers were interested in principle in buying their building freehold. The Towers, formerly a Victorian hotel constructed in 1892 which was converted in the 1940s into a teacher training college, had been renovated and transformed in 2000 into a residential building by their landlord, a local property developer. In 2001, the landlord constructed The Turret, a modern, purpose-built apartment block also near the sea front. A significant proportion of leaseholders in The Turret were senior citizens who were not interested in buying their building freehold.

Hidden and Fuke hired a specialist consultant to advise them on the process of buying one's freehold through the process of right of first refusal. They said that they needed to learn quickly about leaseholder rights in the area and to find out whether the landlord's notice had followed proper procedure. As a result, they discovered that the landlord's notice was invalid on at least two points, including having incorrectly identified the building freehold that the landlord wanted to sell.

The leaseholders at The Towers also discovered that the landlord had incorrectly identified the freeholder company, since details given did not match the records on file at HM Land Registry. With this information in hand, Hidden and Fuke wrote to the landlord, told him that his Section 5 Notice was invalid and told him to send a corrected notice letter to the leaseholders.

The landlord subsequently sent a new Section 5 Notice to the leaseholders, this time offering to sell the freehold of The Towers to leaseholders for £28,500. While leaseholders do not have a right by law to demand that a landlord negotiate on the price of a freehold in a right of first refusal process, the residents at The Towers managed to reach agreement with the landlord on a lower price of £22,500.

The benefits of leaseholder action

By acting quickly, Hidden and Fuke were able to prevent the landlord from selling the freehold of their building to a third party. Under right of first refusal rules, the landlord must offer leaseholders the right to buy at the asking price and the freehold cannot be sold to any other entity until the right of first refusal process has been completed. When Hidden and Fuke got expert advice from the specialist consultant and then notified the landlord that his initial Section 5 Notice was invalid, they bought valuable extra time for leaseholders to get organised and decide whether they wanted to buy the freehold.

The problems to avoid

Hidden and Fuke said that it was important for leaseholders in a building to talk to one another and identify common priorities and goals. Since enfranchisement legislation provides the right for leaseholders to buy the freehold of their own building, but not other buildings, they said that residents should not become distracted by the fact that leaseholders in a nearby building have different priorities and may not want to buy their freehold. Hidden and Fuke advised leaseholders to steer clear of solicitors that lacked specialist expertise and experience in the area of collective enfranchisement and the right of first refusal. 'We had a meeting with one totally useless solicitor, who simply told us what we had told him,' Hidden said. 'This was a real waste of time.'

The lessons learned

Leaseholders at The Towers were able to negotiate successfully with the landlord on the purchase of their building freehold because they remained focused and did not panic when they first received the Section 5 Notice. Hidden and Fuke said that it was important for leaseholders not to feel intimidated when they received this type of legal document from the landlord. But they said that it was essential for leaseholders to act quickly and get the expert advice needed. Leaseholders need to be equipped with solid knowledge of their rights in this highly technical area of residential property law. 'We would have had real problems if we had not hired a specialist consultant to help us. Everything we learned about the right of first refusal process, we learned from that consultant,' Hidden said.

Case study D: The right to manage

Background information

Residents living in a three-storey Victorian house in Hampstead filed the first ever application in London for the right to manage (RTM) in 2004. The house had been converted years earlier into four flats. Three flats were owned by leaseholders and the fourth flat, in the basement, was rented from the landlord by regulated tenants. The three leaseholders, with flats valued at £400,000 to £500,000, had more than 100 years left on their leases and were paying an annual £75 in ground rent. In 2003, they had watched with interest as the new RTM legislation took effect, a year after the passage of the Commonhold and Leasehold Reform Act 2002. They had decided to gain RTM because they had already been managing the property themselves for years on an ad hoc basis and were tired of paying the landlord management fees for this. 'If the stairs needed painting, we just decided what to do amongst ourselves,' said Philippa Ingram, one of the leaseholders. When external work on the building was needed, it had proven simpler and cheaper for the leaseholders to organise the work themselves. When the house needed a new roof, the leaseholders, with the landlord's permission, hired and paid the contractor, and employed a surveyor to inspect the completed work. The residents were also fed up with having to pay the landlord for the right to make certain improvements on their flats. The leaseholders ruled out buying the freehold as an immediate option because they wanted to avoid potentially having to buy the landlord-owned flat in the basement, which was owned by long-standing regulated tenants.

What happened

In early 2004, the leaseholders set up the required RTM company. Then they began the formal RTM process, which took a total of seven months. In February 2004, the RTM company served notice on the landlord, advising that the leaseholders were claiming the right to take over the management of the building. In March, the landlord served a counter-notice in which he challenged the leaseholders' right to get RTM. His grounds were that the house had five flats rather than four and that leaseholders did not have the required numbers for RTM. In April, the leaseholders applied to the LVT to decide. The LVT sent written instructions of all the paperwork to be supplied and asked for 'a written response to the allegation that the RTM company was not on the relevant date entitled to acquire the right to manage the premises'. It was made clear that everything would be copied and sent to the landlord. Ingram, who was the longest-standing resident in the building, prepared a response of about 1,200 words together with the relevant documents. She also requested that the Tribunal visit the building. On 27 April 2004, the LVT notified both parties in writing that there would be a hearing on 26 May. At this point the Tribunal also directed the landlord to prepare a bundle of documents supporting his case and to send four copies to the Tribunal and one to the applicant by 12 May. However, at the 26 May hearing, the landlord arrived with a large stack of documents that had not been sent to the Tribunal or the leaseholders. Ingram, who was representing the RTM company, looked over the documents for half an hour and then requested an adjournment, which was granted. The hearing was rescheduled for 7 June, which gave Ingram time to prepare a short written response to the landlord's documents.

The landlord's case was that there were five flats in the building, not four, since two storerooms in the basement supposedly constituted a fifth flat. On 7 June, before the hearing, the two members of the LVT panel inspected the house in the presence of the landlord and Ingram. They saw that the two cellar storerooms had no windows, no ventilation, no toilet, no running water, no kitchen and were otherwise not set up as an inhabitable dwelling. At the hearing the landlord also said that the RTM company had not been properly set up and that Ingram was not authorised to represent the RTM company at the hearing. In a 10 June written decision sent to both parties, the LVT panel said that the leaseholders did indeed have the right to RTM. The panel said that the RTM company had been properly set up, Ingram was authorised to represent the company and the two cellar storerooms did not represent a flat. Following the decision, the landlord had 21 days in which to appeal. Since he did not do so, the leaseholders' RTM took effect three months later, in September 2004.

The benefits of the right to manage

Ingram said that it was a relief for her and fellow leaseholders to gain the official right to take over the management of their building, thus formalising a management situation that had existed for some years. They were pleased to eliminate the unnecessary management fee and made a substantial saving on building insurance after changing insurer. 'It was well worth doing. It was not very difficult,' she said. Ingram said she had found the LVT extremely efficient and helpful. 'They kept to the point and were very fair to both sides,' she said.

The problems to avoid

Ingram described the RTM process as relatively straightforward and cost-effective, as compared to buying the freehold of a building. The three participants each spent about £125 to cover the cost of hiring a company formation specialist to set up the RTM company. They used Jordans Limited, which charges a flat fee to set up an RTM company, provides the prescribed Memorandum and Articles of Association, and files the necessary documents with Companies House.

The initial paperwork required for setting up the company took a few days and Ingram dedicated about two weeks to preparing paperwork for the Tribunal. As a journalist she had no hesitation in researching and documenting leaseholders' legal rights, but she said it was essential to have at least one person willing and able to do this research, and, if needed, to prepare a case for the LVT. 'Even though the Tribunal is not a court of law, even basic legal experience, which I did not have, would be very useful. I did try to set out our case as simply as possible and to anticipate obvious objections and eliminate logical flaws,' she said. Ingram said landlords could have an advantage over residents because they were generally far more familiar with LVT procedures. She said that leaseholders also needed to take care to set up their RTM company properly, since this was a process that could be challenged by landlords. She and her neighbours were pleased to have outsourced this company formation work to Jordans. It had saved time and the leaseholders were confident that it had been done correctly.

The lessons learned

Ingram said that she had kept a careful record of all correspondence with the landlord and related documents about the building over the years and this had proven a great advantage. The leaseholders were able to challenge the landlord's claim regarding the two cellar storerooms by providing documentation that showed he applied years earlier for local planning permission to convert the storerooms into a flat, but had never had the required work done. 'Corporate memory is important, especially when you have people moving away and new leaseholders arriving,' said Ingram.

While RTM was not going to solve all the disadvantages of leasehold, she said that it gave leaseholders legitimate control over day-to-day issues involving their property. 'It is essentially a practical step forward,' she said.

APPENDIX 3

Enfranchisement notice

There is no specific form prescribed by law for leaseholders wishing to serve notice that they are compelling their landlord to sell them the freehold of their building. However, certain information must be contained in the notice. The following is a template that may be used by leaseholders.

Initial notice by qualifying tenants

Under the Leasehold Reform, Housing and Urban Development Act 1993
Part I, Chapter I, Section 13

Re: *[address of building]*

To: *[name of landlord]* of *[address of landlord]* (Reversioner)

This is an official Collective Enfranchisement notice from the participating qualifying tenants of *[name and address of the building]*, a list of whom is provided in the attached Schedule (Participating tenants).

1. The premises of which the freehold is proposed to be acquired under Section 1(1) of the Act are outlined in *[identify colour]* on the attached plan and known as: *[name and address of the building]*.

2. The premises of which the freehold is proposed to be acquired by virtue of Section 1(1) of the Act are outlined in *[identify colour]* on the

attached plan and known as: *[identify any garages, driveways, pathways, gardens and storage units]* at *[name of building]*.

3. (a) The property over which it is proposed that the rights set out in 3(b) should be granted under Section 13(3)(a)(iii) of the Act are shown outlined in *[identify colour]* on the attached plan.

 (b) The rights referred to in the preceding paragraph are: *[identify, for instance, rights of way on foot and by vehicle, rights of support and protection]*.

4. The grounds upon which it is claimed that the specified premises are premises to which Part I, Chapter I of the Act applies are:

 (a) they consist of a self-contained building or part of a building;

 (b) they contain two or more flats held by qualifying tenants;

 (c) the total number of flats held by qualifying tenants is not less than two-thirds of the total number of flats contained in the premises;

 (d) the total number of participating flat lessees is 50 per cent of all the flats in the premises.

5. The leasehold interest proposed to be acquired under or by virtue of Section 2(1)(a) or (b) of the Act is: *[complete as relevant]*.

6. The flats or other units contained in the specified premises in relation to which it is considered that requirements in Part II of Schedule 9 are applicable are as follows: *[complete as relevant]*.

7. The proposed purchase price is:

 £ *[insert offer price for freehold]* for the freehold interest in the specified premises.

 £ *[insert offer price for other property, if relevant]* for the property within paragraph 2 of this notice.

 For the leasehold interest(s) within paragraph 5 of this notice: £ *[insert offer price, if relevant]*.

8. The full names of all the qualifying tenants of flats in the specified premises, with the addresses of their flats and the particulars required by the Act, are as follows:

(a) Full name of tenant: See Column 1 of the attached Schedule.

(b) Address of tenant: The Flat identified in Column 2 of the attached Schedule (unless otherwise stated in Column 1).

(c) Address of tenant's flat: See Column 2 of the Schedule.

(d) Details of lease:

(e) Date: See Column 3 of the Schedule.

(f) Parties: Lessor: *[name of landlord]* (unless otherwise stated in Column 4 of the Schedule) and Lessee: see Column 4 of the Schedule and any third-party details of whom are set out in Column 4 of the Schedule.

(g) Term: *[number of years in term of lease, from the beginning]* years.

(h) Commencement of term: *[date on which lease originally commenced]*.

(i) Particulars of property (if different from address of flat): See Column 5 of the Schedule.

9. The full name of the person appointed to act as the Nominee Purchaser for the purpose of Section 15 of the Act is: *[name of nominee purchaser]*.

10. The address to which notices should be sent to the Nominee Purchaser under Part I, Chapter II of the Act is: *[name and address of enfranchisers' solicitor in England or Wales]*.

11. The date by which you must respond to this notice by giving a counter-notice under Section 21 is: *[deadline date]*.

12. Copies of this notice are being sent to the following relevant landlords:

Dated _____

Signed _____

Participating qualifying tenants:

Name of participating qualifying tenant	Signature of participating qualifying tenant
Name of leaseholder 1	
Name of leaseholder 2	
Name of leaseholder 3	
Name of leaseholder 4	
Name of leaseholder 5	
Name of leaseholder 6	
Name of leaseholder 7	
Name of leaseholder 8	
Name of leaseholder 9	
Name of leaseholder 10	
Name of leaseholder 11	
Name of leaseholder 12	

THE SCHEDULE

Name of qualifying tenant	Flat number	Date of lease	Lessee as in lease	Any additional property in lease	Status of tenant
Name	*Flat no.*	*Date on which lease commenced*	*Name of lessee in lease*		*Participating or non-participating*
"	"	"	"	"	"
"	"	"	"	"	"
"	"	"	"	"	"
"	"	"	"	"	"
"	"	"	"	"	"
"	"	"	"	"	"
"	"	"	"	"	"
"	"	"	"	"	"
"	"	"	"	"	"
"	"	"	"	"	"

Participation agreement

There is no legal requirement for leaseholders to use a participation agreement when they are enfranchising their building. It is, however, strongly recommended, especially if the building has more than two or three flats. If enfranchisers wish to create a participation agreement, there is no form that is prescribed by law. The following is a template that may be used by leaseholders, regarding a fictional building called Acacia Mansions.

Participation agreement

Enfranchisement of *Acacia Mansions*

This agreement is made on *[date]* between *Acacia Mansions Limited* of *[registered address of nominee purchaser company]* (the 'Nominee Purchaser') and the participating qualifying tenants of *Acacia Mansions, 100 Long Street, London W11 5RR.*

1. This agreement is made in accordance with the Leasehold Reform, Housing and Urban Development Act 1993, referred to here as 'the Act'.

2. It is the intention of the Nominee Purchaser to purchase the freehold of *Acacia Mansions, 100 Long Street, London W11 5RR* in a collective enfranchisement on behalf of the participating tenants of *Acacia Mansions*, a block of 30 flats, referred to here as 'the block'.

3. Each tenant confirms and guarantees that:

(a) he or she is a qualifying tenant according to Section 5 of the Act of a flat in the block and will provide the Nominee Purchaser with Land Registry Office Copy Entries and a copy of the registered lease within seven days of a written request;

(b) he or she does not know of any court order preventing the tenant from participating in the collective enfranchisement;

(c) he or she will inform the Nominee Purchaser in writing within ten days of any change in (a) and (b) above;

(d) he or she will not buy or otherwise acquire any other leasehold flat in the block without first advising the Nominee Purchaser in writing within seven days.

4. The Nominee Purchaser has prepared and will serve upon the freeholder and any other relevant persons the appropriate notices to enfranchise and will register the initial notice as a caution with HM Land Registry and has complied or will comply with the procedure according to the Act.

5. The Nominee Purchaser has instructed *[name of solicitors' firm and address in England or Wales]* and *[name of surveyor]* to advise on the preparation of the enfranchisement notices and other areas of compliance with the Act.

6. The Nominee Purchaser will inform the freeholder of any agreement reached with any non-participating tenant, in accordance with Section 18 of the Act.

7. A reasonable time after completion of the freehold purchase, the Nominee Purchaser will grant, and each participating tenant will accept and execute, a counterpart of a lease of the respective flat and any related property and will surrender the existing lease, details of which are provided in the Schedule below.

8. Each tenant agrees that, if he or she sells or otherwise assigns his or her leasehold flat in the block before the completion of the freehold purchase, that he or she will ensure that the purchaser or assignee of the lease will:

(a) elect to participate in the collective enfranchisement of the block;

(b) give the Nominee Purchaser notice of intention to be bound by this participation agreement and to participate within 14 days of the assignment;

(c) take up the tenant's share in the Nominee Purchaser.

9. (a) In this agreement 'each tenant's share of the freehold price' means the appropriate pro rata number of shares held in the Nominee Purchaser by each participating tenant.

(b) The price to be paid for each new lease, after the freehold purchase, will not be more than each tenant's respective share of the freehold price and the lease will be in reasonable modern form for a term of 999 years.

(c) Each tenant will pay a deposit of ten per cent of the freehold price to the Nominee Purchaser or its solicitor agent, to be used for the deposit when the exchange of contract takes place for the freehold purchase.

(d) Upon completion each tenant will pay to the Nominee Purchaser:

(i) the balance of the tenant's pro rata share of the freehold price;

(ii) all outstanding ground rent and service charges and other payments due under the old lease;

(iii) the appropriate pro rata share of legal, surveyor and other costs incurred by the Nominee Purchaser in the enfranchisement;

(iv) for the shares in the Nominee Purchaser (at par).

10. This agreement does not represent a partnership agreement.

Name of participating qualifying tenant	Signature of participating qualifying tenant
[print name]	[personal signature]

THE SCHEDULE

Name of qualifying tenant	Flat number	Date of lease	Lessee as in lease	Status of tenant
Name	*Flat no.*	*Date on which lease commenced*	*Name of original lessee shown on lease*	*Participating or non-participating*
"	"	"	"	"
"	"	"	"	"
"	"	"	"	"
"	"	"	"	"
"	"	"	"	"
"	"	"	"	"
"	"	"	"	"
"	"	"	"	"
"	"	"	"	"
"	"	"	"	"

APPENDIX 5

Relativity table

Leasehold values as a proportion of freehold value

Lease length remaining (years)	2002 enfranchisable %	Lease length remaining (years)	2002 enfranchisable %
125	98.1	79	92.0
99	97.6	78	91.7
98	97.4	77	91.4
97	97.1	76	91.1
96	96.9	75	90.8
95	96.6	74	90.4
94	96.3	73	90.1
93	96.1	72	89.7
92	95.8	71	89.4
91	95.5	70	89.1
90	95.3	69	88.7
89	95.0	68	88.3
88	94.7	67	88.0
87	94.4	66	87.6
86	94.1	65	87.2
85	93.9	64	86.8
84	93.6	63	86.4
83	93.3	62	86.0
82	93.0	61	85.6
81	92.7	60	85.2
80	92.4	59	84.8

Source: Savills Research

Lease length remaining (years)	2002 enfranchisable %	Lease length remaining (years)	2002 enfranchisable %
58	84.4	31	68.9
57	84.0	30	68.1
56	83.5	29	67.2
55	83.1	28	66.4
54	82.6	27	65.5
53	82.2	26	64.5
52	81.7	25	63.6
51	81.2	24	62.6
50	80.7	23	61.5
49	80.2	22	60.4
48	79.7	21	59.3
47	79.2	20	58.0
46	78.7	19	56.8
45	78.1	18	55.4
44	77.6	17	54.0
43	77.0	16	52.5
42	76.4	15	50.9
41	75.8	14	49.2
40	75.2	13	47.4
39	74.6	12	45.4
38	73.9	11	43.2
37	73.3	10	40.9
36	72.6	9	38.3
35	71.9	8	35.4
34	71.2	7	32.1
33	70.4	6	28.2
32	69.7	5	23.7

APPENDIX 6

Present value table

The present value table shows how much £1 at the present time is worth over a number of years when applying different yields, with interest compounded annually.

Present value of £1 to be paid in future

Years	5.0%	5.5%	6.0%	6.5%
1	0.952381	0.947867	0.943396	0.938967
2	0.907029	0.898452	0.889996	0.881659
3	0.863838	0.851614	0.839619	0.827849
4	0.822702	0.807217	0.792094	0.777323
5	0.783526	0.765134	0.747258	0.729881
6	0.746215	0.725246	0.704961	0.685334
7	0.710681	0.687437	0.665057	0.643506
8	0.676839	0.651599	0.627412	0.604231
9	0.644609	0.617629	0.591898	0.567353
10	0.613913	0.585431	0.558395	0.532726
11	0.584679	0.554911	0.526788	0.500212
12	0.556837	0.525982	0.496969	0.469683
13	0.530321	0.498561	0.468839	0.441017
14	0.505068	0.472569	0.442301	0.414100
15	0.481017	0.447933	0.417265	0.388827
16	0.458112	0.424581	0.393646	0.365095
17	0.436297	0.402447	0.371364	0.342813
18	0.415521	0.381466	0.350344	0.321890

19	0.395734	0.361579	0.330513	0.302244
20	0.376889	0.342729	0.311805	0.283797
21	0.358942	0.324862	0.294155	0.266476
22	0.341850	0.307926	0.277505	0.250212
23	0.325571	0.291873	0.261797	0.234941
24	0.310068	0.276657	0.246979	0.220602
25	0.295303	0.262234	0.232999	0.207138

Present value of £1 to be paid in future

Years	7.0%	7.5%	8.0%	8.5%
1	0.934579	0.930233	0.925926	0.921659
2	0.873439	0.865333	0.857339	0.849455
3	0.816298	0.804961	0.793832	0.782908
4	0.762895	0.748801	0.735030	0.721574
5	0.712986	0.696559	0.680583	0.665045
6	0.666342	0.647962	0.630170	0.612945
7	0.622750	0.602755	0.583490	0.564926
8	0.582009	0.560702	0.540269	0.520669
9	0.543934	0.521583	0.500249	0.479880
10	0.508349	0.485194	0.463193	0.442285
11	0.475093	0.451343	0.428883	0.407636
12	0.444012	0.419854	0.397114	0.375702
13	0.414964	0.390562	0.367698	0.346269
14	0.387817	0.363313	0.340461	0.319142
15	0.362446	0.337966	0.315242	0.294140
16	0.338735	0.314387	0.291890	0.271097
17	0.316574	0.292453	0.270269	0.249859
18	0.295864	0.272049	0.250249	0.230285
19	0.276508	0.253069	0.231712	0.212244
20	0.258419	0.235413	0.214548	0.195616
21	0.241513	0.218989	0.198656	0.180292
22	0.225713	0.203711	0.183941	0.166167
23	0.210947	0.189498	0.170315	0.153150
24	0.197147	0.176277	0.157699	0.141152
25	0.184249	0.163979	0.146018	0.130094

Present value of £1 to be paid in future

Years	9.0%	9.5%	10.0%	10.5%
1	0.917431	0.913242	0.909091	0.904977
2	0.841680	0.834011	0.826446	0.818984
3	0.772183	0.761654	0.751315	0.741162
4	0.708425	0.695574	0.683013	0.670735
5	0.649931	0.635228	0.620921	0.607000
6	0.596267	0.580117	0.564474	0.549321
7	0.547034	0.529787	0.513158	0.497123
8	0.501866	0.483824	0.466507	0.449885
9	0.460428	0.441848	0.424098	0.407136
10	0.422411	0.403514	0.385543	0.368449
11	0.387533	0.368506	0.350494	0.333438
12	0.355535	0.336535	0.318631	0.301754
13	0.326179	0.307338	0.289664	0.273080
14	0.299246	0.280674	0.263331	0.247132
15	0.274538	0.256323	0.239392	0.223648
16	0.251870	0.234085	0.217629	0.202397
17	0.231073	0.213777	0.197845	0.183164
18	0.211994	0.195230	0.179859	0.165760
19	0.194490	0.178292	0.163508	0.150009
20	0.178431	0.162824	0.148644	0.135755
21	0.163698	0.148697	0.135131	0.122855
22	0.150182	0.135797	0.122846	0.111181
23	0.137781	0.124015	0.111678	0.100616
24	0.126405	0.113256	0.101526	0.091055
25	0.115968	0.103430	0.092296	0.082403

APPENDIX 7
Information request prior to a lease extension

There is no specific form prescribed by law for a leaseholder who wishes to exercise his right to obtain information from the landlord about ownership interests in his flat, when he is preparing to get a lease extension. However, certain information must be contained in the notice. The following is a template that may be used by leaseholders.

Notice

Under the Leasehold Reform, Housing and Urban Development Act 1993 Section 41(1),(2)

Re: *[address of the relevant flat]*

To: *[full name of the immediate landlord or the person that receives rent]*

I *[full name of leaseholder]* am sending this notice as a qualifying tenant of the above flat in accordance with the Leasehold Reform, Housing and Urban Development Act 1993.

You are required under Section 41 of the Act to confirm to me whether you are the owner of the freehold interest in the above flat and if not, to provide me with:

1. the name and address of the freeholder of the above flat;

2. the duration of the leasehold interest of my immediate landlord in the above flat and the extent of the premises on which it subsists;

3. the name and address of every person who has a leasehold interest in the above flat who is superior to that of my immediate landlord, the duration of the interest, and the extent of the premises in which it subsists.

You are also required to inform me whether you have received a notice under Section 13 of the Act regarding my flat, where the claim is still current, or to provide me with a copy of such notice.

If such a notice exists, you are required to inform me of the date on which the Section 13 Notice was given, and the name and address of the Nominee Purchaser appointed for the purposes of Section 15 of the above Act in relation to this claim.

You are required to provide me with the above information within 28 days of receiving this notice.

Signed by _____
[provide personal signature of leaseholder]

Signed by _____
[print name of leaseholder]

Date _____
[insert date]

APPENDIX 8

Lease extension notice

There is no specific form prescribed by law for a leaseholder wishing to serve notice that he is compelling the landlord to sell him a 90-year extension. However, certain information must be contained in the notice. The following is a template that may be used by leaseholders.

Notice of claim

Under the Leasehold Reform, Housing and Urban Development Act 1993 Section 42

Re: *[address of relevant flat]*

To: *[full name of freeholder and, if relevant, any head leaseholder]*

1. I *[full name of leaseholder]* hereby claim a new lease regarding *[full address of flat and other relevant information to identify the property]*.

2. I have been the holder of this lease since *[start date of leaseholder's ownership of the lease]*. The lease originally commenced on *[original start date of lease]* for a period of *[number]* years. The names of the original parties to this lease, as they appear on the lease, are *[name and name]*.

3. I propose to pay £ *[amount]* for the new lease and £ *[amount]* for other amounts under Schedule 13 *[include here a separate amount for each of any intermediate landlords]*.

4. I propose that the new lease have the following terms *[complete as appropriate, with reference to the existing lease].*

5. The person acting for me regarding this claim is *[provide name and address in England or Wales of solicitor or other representative, as appropriate].*

6. The landlord must reply to this claim notice by providing me with a counter-notice by *[date]* at the latest. *[The deadline date must be not less than two months after the date of the serving of the initial notice.]*

7. A copy of this notice claim is being provided to *[names of any other landlords].*

Signed by _____
[provide personal signature of leaseholder]

Signed by _____
[print name of leaseholder]

Date _____
[insert date]

APPENDIX 9

Invitation to participate in right to manage

There is a prescribed wording for inviting residents to join a right to manage company. The prescribed wording is provided here below.

Notice of invitation to participate in right to manage

Commonhold and Leasehold Reform Act 2002 Schedule 1 Regulations 3(2)(j) and 8(1)

To: *[name and address]* (See Note 1 below.)

1. *[name of RTM company]* ('the company'), a private company limited by guarantee, of *[address of registered office]*, and of which the registered number is *[number under Companies Act 1985]*, is authorised by its Memorandum of Association to acquire and exercise the right to manage *[name of premises to which notice relates]* ('the premises'). The company intends to acquire the right to manage the premises.

2. *The company's Memorandum of Association, together with its Articles of Association, accompany this notice.

   *The company's Memorandum of Association, together with its Articles of Association, may be inspected at *[address for inspection]* between *[specify times]*. (See Note 2 below.) At any time within the period of seven days beginning with the day after this notice is given, a copy of the Memorandum of Association and Articles of Association may be ordered from *[specify address]* on payment of *[specify fee]*. (See Note 3 below.)

*Delete one of these statements, as the circumstances require.

3. The names of:

    (a) the members of the company;

    (b) the company's directors; and

    (c) the company's secretary,

    are set out in the Schedule below.

4. The names of the landlord and of the person (if any) who is party to a lease of the whole or any part of the premises otherwise than as landlord or tenant are *[specify]*.

5. Subject to the exclusions mentioned in paragraph 7, if the right to manage is acquired by the company, the company will be responsible for:

    (a) the discharge of the landlord's duties under the lease; and

    (b) the exercise of his powers under the lease;

    with respect to services, repairs, maintenance, improvements, insurance and management.

6. Subject to the exclusion mentioned in paragraph 7(b), if the right to manage is acquired by the company, the company may enforce untransferred tenant covenants. (See Note 4 below.)

7. If the right to manage is acquired by the company, the company will not be responsible for the discharge of the landlord's duties or the exercise of his powers under the lease:

    (a) with respect to a matter concerning only a part of the premises consisting of a flat or other unit not subject to a lease held by a qualifying tenant; or

    (b) relating to re-entry or forfeiture.

8. If the right to manage is acquired by the company, the company will have functions under the statutory provisions referred to in Schedule

7 to the Commonhold and Leasehold Reform Act 2002. (See Note 5 below.)

9. *The company intends to appoint a managing agent within the meaning of Section 30B(8) of the Landlord and Tenant Act 1985. *[If known, give the name and address of the proposed managing agent here. If that person is the current managing agent, that fact must also be stated here.]*

   *The company does not intend to appoint a managing agent within the meaning of Section 30B(8) of the Landlord and Tenant Act 1985. *[If any existing member of the company has qualifications or experience in relation to the management of residential property, give details in the Schedule below.]*

   **Delete one of these statements, as the circumstances require.*

10. If the company gives notice of its claim to acquire the right to manage the premises (a 'claim notice'), a person who is or has been a member of the company may be liable for costs incurred by the landlord and others in consequence of the claim notice. (See Note 6 below.)

11. You are invited to become a member of the company. (See Note 7 below.)

12. If you do not fully understand the purpose or implications of this notice, you are advised to seek professional help.

SCHEDULE

The names of the members of the company are:

_____

[state names of company members]

The names of the company's directors are:

_____

[state directors' names]

The name of the company's secretary is:

_____

[state company secretary's name]

[If applicable, see the second alternative in paragraph 9 above.] The following member*[s]* of the company *[has] [have]* qualifications or experience in relation to the management of residential property: *[give details]*.

Signed by authority of the company:

_____

[Signature of authorised member or officer]

_____

[Insert date]

Notes

1. The notice inviting participation must be sent to each person who is at the time the notice is given a qualifying tenant of a flat in the premises but who is not already, and has not agreed to become, a member of the company. A qualifying tenant is defined in Section 75 of the Commonhold and Leasehold Reform Act 2002 ('the 2002 Act').

2. The specified times must be periods of at least two hours on each of at least three days (including a Saturday or Sunday or both) within the seven days beginning with the day following that on which the notice is given.

3. The ordering facility must be available throughout the seven-day period referred to in Note 2. The fee must not exceed the reasonable cost of providing the ordered copy.

4. An untransferred tenant covenant is a covenant in a tenant's lease that he must comply with, but which can be enforced by the company only by virtue of Section 100 of the 2002 Act.

5. The functions relate to matters such as repairing obligations, administration and service charges, and information to be furnished to tenants. Details may be obtained from the RTM company.

6. If the claim notice is at any time withdrawn, deemed to be withdrawn or otherwise ceases to have effect, each person who is or has been a

member of the company is liable (except in the circumstances mentioned at the end of this note) for reasonable costs incurred by:

(a) the landlord;

(b) any person who is party to a lease of the whole or any part of the premises otherwise than as landlord or tenant; or

(c) a manager appointed under Part 2 of the Landlord and Tenant Act 1987 to act in relation to the premises to which this notice relates, or any premises containing or contained in the premises to which this notice relates;

(d) in consequence of the claim notice.

A current or former member of the company is liable both jointly with the company and every other person who is or has been a member of the company, and individually. However, a former member is not liable if he has assigned the lease by virtue of which he was a qualifying tenant to another person and that other person has become a member of the company.

7. All qualifying tenants of flats contained in the premises are entitled to be members. Landlords under leases of the whole or any part of the premises are also entitled to be members, but only once the right to manage has been acquired by the company. An application for membership may be made in accordance with the company's Articles of Association which, if they do not accompany this notice, may be inspected as mentioned in paragraph 2 of the notice.

8. If the right to manage is acquired by the company, the company must report to any person who is landlord under a lease of the whole or any part of premises any failure to comply with any tenant covenant of the lease unless, within the period of three months beginning with the day on which the failure to comply comes to the attention of the company:

(a) the failure has been remedied;

(b) reasonable compensation has been paid in respect of the failure; or

(c) the landlord has notified the company that it need not report to him failures of the description of the failure concerned.

9. If the right to manage is acquired by the company, the management functions of a person who is party to a lease of the whole or any part of the premises otherwise than as landlord or tenant will become functions of the company. The company will be responsible for the discharge of that person's duties under the lease and the exercise of his powers under the lease, with respect to services, repairs, maintenance, improvements, insurance and management. However, the company will not be responsible for matters concerning only a part of the premises consisting of a flat or other unit not subject to a lease held by a qualifying tenant, or relating to re-entry or forfeiture.

10. If the right to manage is acquired by the company, the company will be responsible for the exercise of the powers relating to the grant of approvals to a tenant under the lease, but will not be responsible for the exercise of those powers in relation to an approval concerning only a part of the premises consisting of a flat or other unit not subject to a lease held by a qualifying tenant.

Crown Copyright material is reproduced in this book with the permission of the Controller of HMSO and the Queen's Printer for Scotland.

APPENDIX 10

Right to manage notice

There is a prescribed form by which residents serve notice on their landlord that they are claiming the right to manage their building. The prescribed form is provided here below.

Claim notice for right to manage

Commonhold and Leasehold Reform Act 2002

To *[name and address]* (See Note 1 below.)

1. *[Name of RTM company]* ('the company'), of *[address of registered office]*, and of which the registered number is *[number under Companies Act 1985]*, in accordance with Chapter 1 of Part 2 of the Commonhold and Leasehold Reform Act 2002 ('the 2002 Act') claims to acquire the right to manage *[name of premises to which notice relates]* ('the premises').

2. The company claims that the premises are ones to which Chapter 1 of the 2002 Act applies on the grounds that *[state grounds]*. (See Note 2 below.)

3. The full names of each person who is both:

    (a) the qualifying tenant of a flat contained in the premises; and

    (b) a member of the company;

    and the address of his flat are set out in Part 1 of the Schedule below.

4. There are set out, in Part 2 of the Schedule, in relation to each person named in Part 1 of the Schedule:

    (a) the date on which his lease was entered into;

    (b) the term for which it was granted;

    (c) the date of commencement of the term;

    (d) *such other particulars of his lease as are necessary to identify it.

    *(d) may be ignored if no other particulars need to be given.

5. If you are:

    (a) a landlord under a lease of the whole or any part of the premises;

    (b) party to such a lease otherwise than as landlord or tenant; or

    (c) a manager appointed under Part 2 of the Landlord and Tenant Act 1987 to act in relation to the premises, or any premises containing or contained in the premises;

    you may respond to this claim notice by giving a counter-notice under Section 84 of the 2002 Act. A counter-notice must be in the form set out in Schedule 3 to the Right to Manage (Prescribed Particulars and Forms) (England) Regulations 2003. It must be given to the company, at the address in paragraph 1, not later than *[specify date not earlier than one month after the date on which the claim notice is given]*. If you do not fully understand the purpose or implications of this notice, you are advised to seek professional help.

6. The company intends to acquire the right to manage the premises on *[specify date, being at least three months after that specified in paragraph 5]*.

7. If you are a person to whom paragraph 5 applies and:

    (a) you do not dispute the company's entitlement to acquire the right to manage; and

    (b) you are the manager party under a management contract subsisting immediately before the date specified in this notice;

    you must, in accordance with Section 92 (duties to give notice of contracts) of the 2002 Act, give a notice in relation to the contract to the person who is the contractor party in relation to the contract and to the company. (See Note 3 below.)

8. From the date on which the company acquires the right to manage the premises, landlords under leases of the whole or any part of the premises are entitled to be members of the company. (See Note 4 below.)

9. This notice is not invalidated by any inaccuracy in any of the particulars required by Section 80(2) to (7) of the 2002 Act or Regulation 4 of the Right to Manage (Prescribed Particulars and Forms) (England) Regulations 2003. If you are of the opinion that any of the particulars contained in the claim notice are inaccurate, you may notify the company of the particulars in question, indicating the respects in which you think that they are inaccurate.

SCHEDULE

PART 1

FULL NAMES AND ADDRESSES OF PERSONS WHO ARE BOTH QUALIFYING TENANTS AND MEMBERS OF THE COMPANY

[set out here the particulars required by paragraph 3 above]

PART 2

PARTICULARS OF LEASES OF PERSONS NAMED IN PART 1

[set out here the particulars required by paragraph 4 above]

Signed by authority of the company:

[Signature of authorised member or officer]

[Insert date]

Notes

1. A claim notice (a notice in the form set out in Schedule 2 to the Right to Manage (Prescribed Particulars and Forms) (England) Regulations 2003 of a claim to exercise the right to manage specified premises) must be given to each person who, on the date on which the notice is given, is:

(a) a landlord under a lease of the whole or any part of the premises to which the notice relates;

(b) party to such a lease otherwise than as landlord or tenant; or

(c) a manager appointed under Part 2 of the Landlord and Tenant Act 1987 to act in relation to the premises, or any premises containing or contained in the premises.

But notice need not be given to such a person if he cannot be found, or if his identity cannot be ascertained. If that means that there is no one to whom the notice must be given, the company may apply to a Leasehold Valuation Tribunal for an order that the company is to acquire the right to manage the premises. In that case, the procedures specified in Section 85 of the 2002 Act (landlords etc. not traceable) will apply.

2. The relevant provisions are contained in Section 72 of the 2002 Act (premises to which Chapter 1 applies). The company is advised to consider, in particular, Schedule 6 to the 2002 Act (premises excepted from Chapter 1).

3. The terms 'management contract', 'manager party' and 'contractor party' are defined in Section 91(2) of the 2002 Act (notices relating to management contracts).

4. Landlords under leases of the whole or any part of the premises are entitled to be members of the company, but only once the right to manage has been acquired by the company. An application for membership may be made in accordance with the company's Articles of Association, which may be inspected at the company's registered office, free of charge, at any reasonable time.

Crown Copyright material is reproduced in this book with the permission of the Controller of HMSO and the Queen's Printer for Scotland.

APPENDIX 11
Sample residents' association constitution and rules

Constitution and Rules

Residents' Association of *Acacia Mansions*

1. **Name of the Association**

   The name of the Association shall be *The Residents' Association of Acacia Mansions*, hereafter referred to as 'the Association'.

2. **Objects of the Association**

   Objects of the Association shall be to advance and represent the interests of its members in any matters relating to their residence in *Acacia Mansions*.

3. **Membership of the Association**

   (a) Membership shall be open to all tenants, including leaseholders and subtenants, of residential units at *Acacia Mansions*, except the landlord or any agent or employee of the landlord.

   (b) Each member of the Association shall have one vote, except where there is more than one tenant of any flat, in which case those tenants shall be allowed only one vote amongst them.

(c) Each member shall agree to be bound by the Constitution and Rules of the Association.

(d) The amount of the membership subscription shall be resolved by a General Meeting of the Association.

(e) A member's subscription shall fall due for payment on 31 March of each year, except in the founding year when payment will be due within four weeks of the inaugural General Meeting of the Association.

(f) Any member may resign his or her membership by notice to that effect in writing delivered to the Secretary of the Association.

(g) Any member shall cease automatically to be a member on ceasing to be a tenant, including a leaseholder, at *Acacia Mansions*.

4. The Committee of the Association

(a) The Committee shall meet from time to time and be quorate when at least three Committee members, including at least one officer, are present. Reasonable notice shall be given for Committee meetings, which may be called by any member of the Committee.

(b) The Committee shall consist of up to nine members of the Association and its officers shall be a Chairperson, Secretary and Treasurer.

(c) The members of the Committee and its officers shall be elected at each Annual General Meeting of the Association.

(d) Officers and other Committee members shall pledge to make available to Association members any known information regarding *Acacia Mansions* that will or might have a significant impact on Association members.

(e) Nominations for membership of the Committee shall be proposed by one member of the Association and seconded by another before election by hand vote at the Annual General Meeting.

(f) Nominees elected shall hold their position until the following Annual General Meeting at which time they shall be eligible for re-election to the same position without re-nomination.

(g) The Committee shall have the power to fill any vacancy occurring on the Committee or amongst the officers for the remainder of any term of office without election. It may also co-opt five additional members if deemed necessary or desirable.

(h) The Committee may appoint one or more subcommittees from amongst the membership provided that any decisions of a subcommittee shall be subject to ratification by the Committee.

(i) In the event of a tied vote at a Committee meeting, the Chairperson or acting Chairperson shall be entitled to make a casting vote.

5. Meetings of the Association

(a) Except in its founding year, the Association shall conduct an Annual General Meeting not later than *[date]* in that year.

(b) An extraordinary General Meeting of the Association may be called at any time by the Secretary, either at the written request of no fewer than three members or upon written instruction of the Committee.

(c) An ordinary General Meeting of the Association may be called at any time by the Secretary.

(d) A minimum of 14 days' notice in writing shall be given to the members of any General Meeting of the Association. The agenda for any General Meeting shall accompany any notice of it.

6. Resolutions and Voting

(a) A record of all resolutions or nominations to be put at a General Meeting, together with the names of their proposers and seconders, shall be kept by the Secretary and be available for viewing by any member of the Association.

(b) Voting at any meeting of the Association or of its Committee or of any subcommittee shall be by a show of hands unless a majority demands otherwise. A simple majority of those voting shall decide any issue. Where a majority cannot be obtained, the Chairperson shall have a casting vote.

(c) In the case of matters concerning Sections 18 to 30 of the Landlord and Tenant Act 1985 ('service charges'), only those members of the Association liable to pay the variable service charge in question shall be eligible to vote.

(d) Any member may by notice in writing to the Chairperson authorise another member to attend meetings and vote on behalf of that member in his or her absence. Any member acting on behalf of another member shall be counted in both capacities in the calculation of a quorum. No such substitution shall be allowed at meetings of the Committee or subcommittees.

7. Financial Matters

(a) The Association shall maintain a bank account, all cheques drawn against which shall be signed by an officer of the Association and one other member of the Committee.

(b) All funds and any other property of the Association shall be held and administered by the Committee.

(c) The Treasurer shall present a Statement of Account and a Balance Sheet for the preceding financial year to each Annual General Meeting for which purpose the financial year shall end on 31 March.

(d) Auditors (who may not also be members of the Committee) may be appointed by resolution at an Annual General Meeting.

(e) In the event of the Association being dissolved, any surplus funds shall be distributed evenly amongst the members at the time.

8. Constitution and Rules

No changes shall be made to the Constitution and Rules except at the Annual General Meeting or at an extraordinary General Meeting convened for the purpose nor shall they be suspended.

Index

This index covers chapters, Glossary and Appendices. Entries categorise parties involved in buying, selling, managing and inhabiting properties, freeholds and leaseholds. An 'f.' after a page number indicates a figure, or figure and text; a 't.' indicates a table, or table and text.

scope 112
third-party sales, criminal offences 122-3
timeframes
    at auction 119-20t.
    deemed withdrawals 122
    incentives 119t.
withdrawals
    costs 120, 122
    scope 121
right-to-enfranchise (RTE) companies 56
right to manage *see* RTM
rights granted and excepted 17
RMCs (resident management companies) 23, 45, 161
    board of directors 141, 158
    cessation 138, 139
    collective enfranchisement from 139
    outsourcing by 140-1
    professionalism 139-40
    residents' associations and 138-9
    see also nominee purchasers
RPTS (Residential Property Tribunal Service) 33-4, 134
    scope 100
    structure 100-2f.
    see also Rent Assessment Panels
RTE (right-to-enfranchise) companies 56
RTM (right to manage) 38
    alternatives to 98
    buildings qualifications 88-9
    case study 175-8
    cessation 96
    collective enfranchisement and 88, 97-8
    completion
        constraints from 93
        participants 92, 96
        process 92-3
    costs 93-4
    DIY management and managing agents 97
        case study 167, 168, 169
    extension of leases and 98
    formal agreement 95
    incentives 88
    landlord's counter-notice 91-2
    limitations 87
    participants 89, 90